UNDERSTANDING YOUR SOCIAL AGENCY

SECOND EDITION

SAGE HUMAN SERVICES GUIDES, VOLUME 3

SAGE HUMAN SERVICES GUIDES

A series of books edited by ARMAND LAUFFER and CHARLES D. GARVIN. Published in cooperation with the University of Michigan School of Social Work and other organizations.

A **SAGE** HUMAN SERVICES GUIDE **3**

UNDERSTANDING YOUR SOCIAL AGENCY

SECOND EDITION

Armand LAUFFER

Published in cooperation with the University of Michigan School of Social Work

SAGE PUBLICATIONS
The International Professional Publishers
Newbury Park   London   New Delhi

SAGE Publications, Inc.
2455 Teller Road
Newbury Park, California 91320

SAGE Publications Ltd.
6 Bonhill Street
London EC2A 4PU
United Kingdom

SAGE Publications India Pvt. Ltd.
M-32 Market
Greater Kailash I
New Delhi 110 048 India

Printed in the United States of America

Library of Congress Cataloging in Publication Data

Lauffer, Armand.
  Understanding your social agency (second edition).

  (Sage human services guides ; v. 3)
  1. Social service—Handbooks, manuals, etc.
2. Organization—Handbooks, manuals, etc.
I. Title II. Series.
HV35.U5 1984   361   84-18014
ISBN 0-8039-2349X (pbk.)

93 94 10

CONTENTS

To Orly and Josh

whose understanding deepens

to wisdom as they continue *tshuvah*

PREFACE AND
ACKNOWLEDGMENTS

Most acknowledgments begin with references to those whose aid and support were invaluable to the author. These I will make momentarily. But first I want to make a rather unusual acknowledgment.

There isn't a single new idea in this second edition of *Understanding Your Social Agency,* nor were there any new ideas in the first edition when it came out in 1977! So why publish it in the first place? And why publish it again in an expanded version with three additional chapters and nearly twice the number of original pages? The answers to both questions are the same and they are different. I'll explain.

An earlier version of UYSA was developed at the University of Michigan's Continuing Education Program in the Human Services under a grant from the state's Office of Substance Abuse Services and later expanded through a grant from the Edna McConnel Clark Foundation. At the time, my co-authors and I were concerned with providing access to concepts about organizations and how they work to social agency practitioners. The idea was to help those practitioners translate behavioral science concepts into action guides they could use to improve both the quality and scope of service delivery.

When Sage decided to publish UYSA a few years later, it had been fully tested with feedback from hundreds of users suggesting some needed revisions and some additions. These we made. We had expected only modest interest, so the responses from new readers took us somewhat by surprise. It quickly became the leading seller in the *Human Services Guides* series, having gone through seven printings in its first seven years. Along with the expanded readership came expanded usage of the book.

In addition to agency practitioners who continued to purchase it and use it as an action guide, college and university instructors ordered it for their students as supplementary reading in some courses and as the core text in others. It has been ordered by more than 600 college book stores for community college courses; for undergraduate sociology, social work, and human service courses; and for use in graduate and professional schools of social work, business, public health, and nursing. "But why?" we wondered, since there was nothing new in the book.

We had designed it to *demystify* organizations; to take the sometimes arcane literature of sociology and social psychology and to make it accessible to practitioners. We had not intended it as an original contribution to literature. That there was nothing new in the book was by design. We had purposefully selected basic (one might call them *classic and neoclassic*) concepts from the social sciences, essentially drawing from mainstream theorists and their oft-quoted books and published journal articles.

And that, apparently, was precisely what attracted both instructors and students. The first edition of *Understanding Your Social Agency* was used as a key to much of the literature on organizations for both students and practitioners. "My students had been resisting the reading assignments in complex organizations," a colleague wrote, "but they took to UYSA with no difficulty. They saw it as an English translation of jargonese. Once they understood the basic concepts, I had much less difficulty in sending them back to Parsons, Simon, Thompson, Blau, and the others." He then went on to tell me what he thought was missing from the book.

I took his words seriously and did a little informal market analysis of my own, querying both students and faculty who had used the book. And based on their suggestions I have expanded UYSA in a number of ways. First, each of the original chapters has had material added. Chapter 1, in fact, was reshaped to emphasize careers in organizations not just personality styles. The last chapter was expanded to show the relationships between the use of power in organizations and the processes of economic and social exchange. Three new chapters were added to deal with organizational goals, technologies, and people processing and changing activities. That these are not new concepts is their strength. Grounded empirically and subject to heavy review and reexamination, they are at the foundation of our growing knowledge of how social agencies work. I don't mean to imply that other, newer ideas or approaches to organizational analysis have no value. To the contrary; it is my expectation that once readers are familiar with the basics and the original sources on which this volume is supported, they will be able to go on to more contemporary sources independently and with a more critical eye.

For the original idea of the book we all owe thanks to Professor Beth Reed, whose guidance and direction led to completion of the first edition. Lynn Nybell and Carla Overberger not only wrote some of the original chapter drafts, but designed the basic format, which remains unchanged. Professor Lawrence Zeff added immeasurably to the first three chapters. Matt Lampe drafted the first version of the chapter on power relationships. I bear ultimate responsibility for the current version of *UYSA* and for the additional materials. But if real credit is due, it is not to the "translator" but to the theorists and researchers on whom we have drawn liberally.

INTRODUCTION

Eight hours a day, five days a week! That's a heavy commitment of time to put into work. If you are a social worker or anyone else employed in the human services, chances are that most of your time is spent within an organizational context. The context may be that of a social agency, a hospital, a school; these are all formal organizations and often complex ones. Each such organization is bound together by its missions, technologies, formal rules and informal norms, operating procedures, authority structures, and patterns for relation to consumers and resource providers.

If your job is meaningful, if you care about the work you do and the people you do it with (both clients and colleagues), your thoughts about the organization are likely to carry over into non-job related activities. As if forty hours-plus of living within and thinking about a formal organization were not enough, you are undoubtedly also a member, customer, client, and perhaps even a "victim" of many other formal organizations. Within any of these, you may be on one or another rung of some sort of career ladder, working your way into greater responsibility and commitment. Thus perhaps half or more of your waking time is shaped directly by your involvement in one or more organizations.

Living within an organization can be both satisfying and disturbing. Complaints about the red tape and impersonality of a bureaucracy, job stress and burn out, feelings of dependency coupled with frustration; these are all-too-frequent responses to life in the organization. Yet we often also find that life very satisfying—both motivating and fulfilling. The causes and consequences of such feelings are rarely well understood by employees of human service organization. Despite their sensitivity to individual needs and perceptions, social workers are not sufficiently aware of organizational forces that shape and give meaning to those needs and perceptions.

ORGANIZATIONS

This is a book about organizations. Before you can understand your social agency better, you'll have to know how organizations work and what they are. *Organizations are purposeful social units; that is, they are deliberately constructed to achieve certain goals or to perform tasks and conduct programs that might not be as effectively or efficiently performed by individuals or informal groups.* One might say that organizations are the means for achieving certain ends, although some people might argue that, once established, organizations tend to become ends in their own right. There is logic to this position, for just as organizations are resources for meeting the interests of certain publics, they also seek resources to do their work and support their own interests.

But organizations aren't just means and ends. *They are made up of people who perform a variety of tasks in the fulfillment of their many roles within the various offices and positions established within the organization. Their actions are coordinated so that individual outputs are somehow supportive of each other and integrated with the organization's goals.*

Implicit in this definition are a number of norms against which an organization might be judged: purpose (relevance, importance; appropriateness of the organization's construction (structure) in relation to that purpose; goal attainment (effectiveness); efficiency; types of actions and programs performed; the people involved as mandators, staff, consumers (and the status, training, or supervision that might be required for them to perform their roles); the nature of the coordination process with its implications for power and authority relationships. These will be dealt with in Chapters 1 through 10. Implicit also are the two major themes that have dominated the literature on organizations. The first, generally referred to as the "classical school" might more descriptively be called *structural determinism*. It assumes that what organizations do is primarily influenced by their technologies and by their structures. Structural determination focusses attention on division of labor, chain of command, delegation of authority, and obligations. Relationships between people and organizational subunits are perceived to be arranged to accomplish general goals and more specific objectives. Classical theorists assume that tasks can be so organized as to accomplish efficiently what the organization is designed for. Within this conceptualization people's relationships within an organization have no meaning other than those established by the organization. Their goal-oriented behavior (that is, the activities they perform in pursuit of the organization's goals) can be optimized through incentives, training, just treatment, proper supervision—all oriented toward the performance of tasks as specified. This approach in the literature on administration has come to be known as *scientific management*.

But this approach is not scientific at all, according to those who have enunciated the second major theme in organizational theory. These "neoclassicists" are mostly behavioral scientists whose studies suggest that people, not structures, are what give shape and meaning to organizations. Often referred to as the *human relations* school, these behavioral scientists argue that organizations are, and *should* be manipulated to serve people's ends and not the reverse. People are not motivated by economic (rational) considerations alone. The rewards for participation in organization life are frequently social and personal and may have little bearing on the purposes of the organization of which they are members (staff, legitimators, consumers). The emphasis of these theorists is on the natural interests of participants, not on the designed or blue-printed functions to which they may be assigned.

There is yet a third major theme, generally known as the "systems" approach, which has come to be referred to as the *modern* school of organizational theory. This approach focuses on the interrelationships of the (1) individual participant, (2) the formal arrangement of organizational functions (the formal organization); (3) the informal roles and norms that emerge out of daily interaction (the informal organization); (4) the forces in the environment (geographic, economic, and sociocultural) that shape organizational goals and provide the organization with necessary legitimacy and resources (inputs) as well as the consumers of its products (outputs); (5) the goals of the organization and technologies it uses to achieve those goals; and (6) the related tasks and functions that must be performed if the organization is to respond to internal and external forces, enabling it to survive and to grow.

If I have taken sides between these points of view, it is in the direction of taking an "open systems" approach. This is not to suggest that I will be presenting a comprehensive picture of how agencies work or that I've come up with a single integrated theory of organizations. To the contrary, the ten perspectives on organizations presented in this book, despite the implications each has for the others, are intended to provide the reader with different viewpoints from which the organization can be examined.

More about these perspectives shortly. First, we should identify what distinguishes *social agencies* from other organizations.

SOCIAL AGENCIES

I have chosen the term "social agency" deliberately to contrast with the more current appellation "human service organization (HSO)''. When I first began my career in social work, there were social agencies, hospitals, prisons, schools, libraries, and other entities that have recently been grouped under the more general designation of HSO. I liked the earlier term and still do. *Social* implies a mission, a purpose, an orientation toward service. "Social agency" was of course, just short for "social *service* agency". *Agency,* in contrast with other forms of *organization,* implies a particular kind of social unit, one that acts in behalf of or in place of others; in this sense, the general public, or sectors within it.

Moreover, while HSO is a term current within the social work profession and among a number of behavioral scientists, it is rarely used by doctors, nurses, librarians, teachers, professors, attorneys, and others who work in human service organizations, but who are content in calling them by other names. I'm not sure why this is so. I suspect that there may be a kind of "imperialism" in the language of social workers, or perhaps the term is a way of avoiding the very troublesome fact that social work technologies may be more indeterminate than those of some of the other professions I mentioned. The imperialism is also evidenced in the multiplicity of settings and host organizations in which social workers are now found (not just in *social* agencies). And it is in those settings where the indeterminacy (lack of close correlation between what social workers do and the end they profess to strive toward) is most evident—where their work may be evaluated in comparison with that of other professions. I don't mean this as a criticism of social work. There are good reasons (explanations) for such indeterminacy, and we will explore them in Chapters 7 and 8.

There is, of course, another very important justification for the HSO designation. By opening a lens wide, it is possible to take in a broader field, and, in so doing, learn more through classification and comparison. For this reason much of my analysis will be drawn from the literature on HSOs and I will occasionally use the term interchangeably with "social agency." Let's look at that literature right now; a great deal of it attempts to spell out how HSOs differ from other organizations.

To illustrate, I'll draw on the work of two of my colleagues at Michigan, Rosemary Sarri and Yeheskel Hasenfeld (1978), who refer to HSOs as *agencies* of the community, broadly defined to include society at large and smaller geographic or interest communities, established for purposes of promoting welfare, education, health, social control, and the preservation of social values mandated by society in order to contribute to the fulfillment of societal (social) functions. Drawing on joint work with two other Michigan colleagues (Robert Vinter, 1963; and Richard English, 1974), they classify HSOs on the basis of the kinds of clients they serve and the activities they perform on those people. Clients can be classified along a continuum from the "most normal" to the "most malfunctioning" (those labeled mentally ill, social deviants, criminals).

So far this may not seem very different from the consumers of other kinds of organizations such as business firms. Don't they also serve all kinds of people? The difference is that people become clients of HSOs specifically because they have been located on such a continuum and have had their characteristics so labeled.

The activities that HSOs perform can be categorized as "people processing" and "people changing," (what Robert Vinter has described as "treatment"). Processing is essentially a program of labeling. It includes intake, diagnosis or assessment, categorization, and referral to others for purposes of action or treatment. Treatment refers to a variety of change strategies aimed at control, education, personal development, and so on.

These are useful designations, and you might keep them in mind as you read on. But they say more about the *what* than the *what for* of these organizations. Around this question a former colleague, David Austin adds considerable clarity. Austin (1981) defines the work of HSOs to be oriented toward the production of public goods, in contrast to industry or private, profit-making organizations that produce or distribute private goods. As public goods, their products (services) are always under some form of public scrutiny, often evaluated differently by distinct interest groups. Some public goods are universal, available to all equally and simultaneously (like air quality control) while other services are available to all, but not necessarily used equally (such as those provided by schools and libraries). Some public goods are categorical, that is they are available only to certain categories of people: the aged, the infirm, the mentally ill, children with special needs. Finally, others are redistributional, reallocating goods and services to those who have not been successful at competing for such resources in the market (examples include social security and welfare grants, public housing).

The *social agencies* I will be referring to throughout this book generally fall into the categorical and redistributional designations of HSOs. Their services include protection, standard of living enhancement, developmental enhancement, and nonfiscal redistribution of resources.

HOW TO USE THE BOOK, AND WHAT FOR

I have divided the book into eleven chapters. Each of the first ten takes a particular perspective or point of view from which to examine an agency. For example, in Chapter 1, we explore what it means to live in the agency eight hours a day and how individuals work out their career patterns within them. Chapters 2 and 3 examine the formal organization of roles and the informal organization of norms and small groups in which human relations are so central. In Chapter 4 we use organization charts to comprehend the formal organization, but begin to examine the often invisible functional links between subunits that are not (officially) connected directly.

Chapter 5 is our first full introduction to systems theory in which the agency is understood to be composed of production (service to clients), adaptive, boundary, and management subsystems. Elements in the boundary system are assessed more fully in Chapter 6, as we look at the ecological factors that influence an organization's goals and the means it has at its disposal. Those means are the focus of Chapter 7, which deals with people changing and people processing, and Chapter 8, which examines the agency as the context within which a number of human service and other organizational technologies are applied.

How those technologies shape an agency's goals and how those goals are further shaped by environmental forces is the subject of Chapter 9. Chapter 10 builds on much of what was presented earlier, but from a different perspective— that of exchange relationships between people and organizational units, and how these exchanges contribute to the establishment of power and authority within the organization and through the organization.

In each of these chapters I have included one or more exercises to give you the opportunity of testing the concepts presented, so as to assess their utility in your work setting. You get a chance to test them all individually and together in Chapter 11, in which I share with you a contingency approach to understanding your social agency, and to making each of the ten perspectives into a problem-solving method.

As this suggests, the book was designed for use by people who work within social agencies or who are in other ways affected by them. You may be more interested in just finding out about social agencies and how they work or in getting a handle on the social science literature that deals with organizations. I think you will find this volume, slim as it is, a helpful introduction. But understand, it is only an introduction and is not intended to substitute for more rigorous and advanced study. I think you will find each chapter both mind-opening and useful. For those of you who have taken formal courses in organizational theory, this book might serve as a review and to reawaken your curiosity and quicken your critical eye.

—Armand Lauffer
Ann Arbor, 1984

Chapter 1

YOUR AGENCY AS A CAREER ARENA

Work and careers are integrally related. The place in which you work is the arena within which career decisions and moves are made. By career, I am referring to the stages and levels of your occupational growth and development. By arena, I mean the place where the action takes place—careers are active processes.

In this chapter we will take the perspective that your agency is a career arena. We'll look at the closeness of fit between your interests and capacities, the opportunities and demands of the agency and those of the profession or occupation you have chosen. We will then examine five fairly typical ways in which agency personnel make their career choices as they work their way up the ladder, box themselves into corners, make lateral moves, or move out of the agency or a particular work unit within it.

AGENCIES, OCCUPATIONS, AND PROFESSIONS

Most of us take career related jobs for a variety of reasons: for income and security; for status and prestige; as an opportunity to fulfill ourselves; or to do something useful for society, to be of benefit to others. These are the same reasons we choose such occupations as counseling and undergo specialized training in order to perform occupational functions and job related tasks. That training often is given in a professional school. Becoming members of a profession provides entry access to a number of occupations. Although there is a close coincidence between professions and occupations, these are not necessarily identical. For example, social workers can become substance abuse counselors, group therapists, or community organizers. Occupations, such as family treatment, may be entered into by persons trained in a number of professions: psychology, social work, psychiatry, or education.

Because careers hold out the promise of continuous advancement (and the rewards that come with advancement), many people are willing to undergo a number of years' training in order to prepare themselves properly, and to take stepping stone or trial work experience jobs, so as to try out different occupational identities at various stages in the career advancement process. In a number of cases such activities require delaying the gratifications of higher paying or more fulfilling jobs. At some point, however, any of us may find ourselves caught between several masters.

As employees, we are accountable to our employers, but as professionals, we may feel ourselves more accountable to the norms and values of our chosen profession or to the clients on whose behalf we practice. As individuals, we have personal goals and needs that may or may not be adequately fulfilled through our occupational pursuits. The extent to which your work within the agency is satisfying and fulfilling will depend to a great extent on the congruity or fit between your interests and capacities and the demands and expectations of both the employer and the profession with which you identify. Some of the variables that can be used to assess the closeness of fit are summarized in the following table.

Table 1
Closeness of Fit Between Worker, Job, and Profession*

You, the Worker	The Agency	The Profession
Knowledge and skill	Tasks and other technical requirements of the job	Competencies in the performance of professional tasks
Personal reward and value hierarchy (e.g., income, security, prestige, fulfillment, etc.)	Capacity of the agency to provide those rewards now or in the foreseeable future	Capacity of the profession to provide such rewards
Ability to cope with stress and ambiguity	Stressfulness or ambiguity integral to the job and availability of mechanisms to deal with them	Expectation that ambiguity is integral to practice and availability of support system to cope with stress
Personality characteristics: tending toward independence or compliance	Extent to which rules govern decision making and worker autonomy	Professional norms of autonomy

*Since both work and profession are interwoven in the occupational choice, I have dealt with only three variables: worker, profession, and work setting. For a more complete discussion of the variables listed, see Lauffer (1982: ch. 4).

If the fit between the agency and the profession is not close around any of these issues, you may find yourself having to do battle to improve things at work, you may choose to leave the job for another in which you can be more professional, or you will have to find some way of accommodating to the agency and its requirements. This may not be all that difficult, particularly if you are fully identified with the agency and its goals and are understanding of its limitations. Things get a bit more complicated when the fit between you and your capacities and those of the agency or the profession are not close.

If there is a mismatch between you and the agency, say in the areas of your knowledge and skill and the technical requirements of the job, this can be corrected if you're willing and have the capacity to learn. If not, you may have to accept limited career opportunities within the agency or seek another more compatible job. Job redesign is another possibility, and a number of agencies have moved in the direction of restructuring jobs to fit the interests and capacities of staff (within the overall mission of the organization). The same is true in the areas of stress management and coping with ambiguity. Staff training, establishment of support groups, and changes in job task specification can do much to correct an otherwise defeating situation.

A poor fit between your values and personality characteristics and the agency's capacity to meet your needs may be harder to correct for. On the value side, it may just not be possible for the organization to accommodate to your income requirements, need for prestige or security, desire to engage in social action. If you can't or won't compromise your interests, and if the agency won't budge, you may have to look elsewhere.

Take a moment now to complete the following exercise.

Step 1: Rank order the items in each column, indi-
cating what you seek in a job and the rewards that
your agency or work setting is capable of
providing you. Add other items we may have left
out.

YOUR REWARD/VALUE HIERARCHY	REWARDS THE AGENCY CAN PROVIDE
_____ Feeling of accomplishment	_____ Opportunity to be successful
_____ Prestige and social standing	_____ Prestige and social standing
_____ Helping others	_____ Opportunities to be helpful
_____ Good working relationships	_____ Positive work-related climate
_____ High income/job security	_____ High income/job security
_____ Overcoming challenges	_____ Challenging work
_____ Professional or self-development	_____ Opportunity to develop

Step 2: How close is the fit? Rate the closeness of fit on a
five-point scale by placing a check (✔) where
appropriate.

High Fit |___|___|___|___| No Fit
      4   3   2   1   0

Step 3: If the fit is not close, what are your
alternatives? Check the ones that you think make
the most sense.

_____ Seek other work   _____ Try to change myself

                              _____ Try to change the agency or

_____ Accept things as they are   _____ Work climate

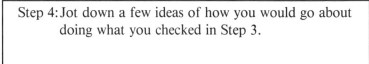

Step 4: Jot down a few ideas of how you would go about doing what you checked in Step 3.

Taken from A. Lauffer (1979).

MATCHING WHAT YOU VALUE WITH WORK-RELATED REWARDS

Now design similar exercises to deal with the other three variables we identified in the preceding table. Fill them in. What have you learned about yourself and the agency? Could you redesign all four exercises to deal with worker-agency *occupation* congruity? How?

When the fit between the individual and the profession is poor, accommodation or change may be more difficult. Although one can't expect a profession to change itself in response to the needs of individual practitioners, there are generally opportunities to find a particular nitch in the profession that fits the individual's capacities or needs. This may require an occupational shift say from direct practice to management. Changing one's aspirations or ability to perform according to the profession's norms is another option. While leaving and entering another field is a third, this can be very costly to the individual when weighed against the years of personal investment in education and the development of a professional identity.

The extreme choices of going through a major personal overhaul, redirecting the agency or changing the profession (perhaps by pioneering a new specialization within it), or leaving one or both, are rarely necessary. Most of us manage with a little adjustment here or there. In fact, successful practitioners and administrators are often those who not only make successful adjustments, but who can use the lack of close fit as a challenge to their ingenuity or creativity. They are often the innovators in both the workplace and professional arenas. After all, it takes a bit of dissatisfaction with what is or a vision of a better state of affairs to want to take the risks that come with innovation and change. Taking risks may also depend on the stage you are at in your career. In the early stages of your career, you are more likely to test out different work settings, different styles of professional and work related behaviors, and to press for changes in the way in which the agency or the profession operates. As you move on, consolidating your gains, you may be a bit less willing to rock the boat, having invested a good deal in your achievements. More about this later, when we explore career styles within an agency setting. First, I want to discuss with you those kinds of agencies where both professional challenges and career opportunities seem to be the greatest.

OPPORTUNITIES FOR CAREER MOBILITY

In some agencies upward mobility is possible; in others there may be greater opportunities to move laterally or horizontally, and in still others there are significant and positive opportunities to move downward with no loss of benefits or prestige.

Upward mobility generally refers to movement into managerial or specialist levels within an organization. Such movements are accompanied by an increase in responsibility and autonomy, better pay and working conditions, more prestige (but sometimes more pressure and job stress, too). Large agencies, particularly those with tall hierarchies (see Chapter 4) in which there are many levels of management, or those in which there is a high ratio between managers and subordinates, afford the greatest opportunities for upward mobility.

But for many professionals such upward mobility is not a goal. Few college professors aspire to become deans or university presidents; most even shy away from becoming department heads. Most school teachers do not aspire to specialists or school principals. Most social workers were trained to be direct service practitioners (with individuals, families, groups, and communities), and they value direct practice. They may aspire to become more skilled and competant therapists, counselors, and organizers, and the professional rewards they receive (prestige earned, a sense of doing what one is qualified for, an opportunity to work out one's social commitments) may be precisely what they aim for. Movement into a managerial role would be diverting at best and more likely perceived as requiring considerable sacrifice.

For these people lateral mobility may be much more appropriate. For a school teacher lateral mobility might entail moving from the classroom in one part of town to a classroom in another part of town where working conditions are considered better or where the challenges are greater. For the social worker it may mean a shift from treating individuals to work in family treatment or from work in protective services for children to protective services for older adults. Such shifts may entail some retraining, but rarely require downgrading in terms of salary or benefits.

Large agencies that provide a wide variety of services or that serve many populations and cover multiple geographic locales provide considerable opportunities for lateral moves. But so do smaller agencies that are in a growth or expansionary phase in their development or that shift their programs and services in response to new needs and opportunities (examples are home health care services for the disabled and women's crisis centers). In some of these settings, in fact, workers may be expected to shift jobs or to perform multiple jobs at a moment's notice. These kinds of organizations generally have flat structures with few or no levels of hierarchy between practitioners and top management.

There are other, stable organizations (with either tall or flat structures) in which great value is placed on the professionalism of the staff (universities, family service agencies, guidance clinics). Here a downward move from administration to direct practice (teaching, research, counseling, treatment) is seen as an opportunity for fulfillment and for advancing the purposes of the organization. No loss of either prestige or income need accompany such moves.

DEALING WITH CHANGE

Career mobility, as the term implies, is a process of change. But not everyone is comfortable with change. Some people, in fact, attempt to protect themselves against change when they perceive it to be against their interests. Almost everyone opposes change if it either reduces the scope and the importance of the tasks assigned them, or if change results in a net reduction of the staff and the resources under their control. Change tends to be resisted by people who have been in their positions for a long time and are comfortable with programs and procedures as they are. Rational arguments about the objective results of a given change are not likely to be as persuasive as arguments that spell out the payoffs or benefits to the parties directly affected by the proposed change.

Change is welcomed when it provides opportunities for advancement and for aggrandizement. The forces for change are strengthened by fluctuation in an agency's external environment. This is particularly true when changes occur in client populations, in funding sources, in public opinion, or in other agencies upon which your agency depends. Those individuals who interact with elements in that environment—intake and outside workers, community agents, case managers, administrators, fund raisers—are the most likely to welcome change and to promote it.

Change is more likely to be generated or supported from within the organization when staff turnover is great or people are moved from one unit to another within the agency; new people join the staff; or staff backgrounds, educational levels, skills and areas of expertise are diverse. Internally generated change is likely to be supported when staff members have been given an opportunity to participate in the design of the change process; the decision to institute a change comes after a gradual and extended process of introduction; similar changes in like organizations have proved rewarding to members of that organization and this information is known; both administrative and charismatic leaders in the organization support (or at least do not oppose) the change.

Turn your attention for a moment to your own agency or to your work unit. How do your supervisors, your subordinates, and your peers react to change? Who activates it? Take a specific example of a policy, programmatic, or procedural change with which you are particularly familiar. Can you describe the behavior of your colleagues in promoting or opposing the change in question? Does the foregoing discussion shed some light on what happened? Knowing what you know now, how would you deal with personnel issues to facilitate a smoother change in policy, program, or procedure?

FIVE CAREER PATTERNS

Anthony Downs, a social scientist with the Urban Institute, describes five career styles common to most complex organizations, each of which is a different response to change (Downs, 1967). I think you will find his analysis instructive and recognize both yourself and many of your colleagues and supervisors within it. He refers to "climbers," "zealots," "advocates," and "statesmen." Before we examine each of these, one at a time, I want to point out that these categories tend to deal primarily with upward mobility within an organizational setting and thus are too limited to serve as a framework for analysis of all aspects of organizational careers. Nevertheless, they do provide some important insights into why people behave as they do in social agencies and other work settings.

The "climber" is on the move up, hopefully, to the top. There are a number of ways in which he or she can get there. The most direct is promotion. One way to improve the odds for promotion is to be recognized as competent at carrying out one's official tasks. Another is to get involved in as many committees and subgroups as possible. If the chances for promotion are relatively small, the climber may resort to aggrandizing his or her area of responsibility. This strategy is often perceived by others as empire building. The more resources under the climber's control, the more influence he or she has within the organization and the more indispensable the climber becomes. The surest way to build an empire is to increase the number of personnel directly under one's control. As the number of subordinates increases, added staff must be justified by absorbing more programs and responsibilities. These may come either from areas previously controlled by other people or from new programs generated by the climber.

When the path to promotion is blocked and when empire building is not feasible, the only route left for a climber may be to jump to another agency, selling personal skill, expertise, and confidence. The only real constraint here is the job market. If there are no jobs available for the climber and all possible contacts made during the empire building process have been tried, then the climber's path may be blocked. The response is often frustration that may be expressed in interpersonal conflict.

In terms of leadership style, the climber tends to closely control subordinates to ensure nobody else is seen as a rising star. This style of leadership often suppresses innovation from below. Nevertheless, the climber believes, rightfully so, that the more change there is, the greater opportunity for advancement of subordinates as well as himself or herself.

The second type is the "conserver" who is in many ways the opposite of the climber. Like climbers, however, conservers tend to be concerned mainly with themselves. Unlike climbers, conservers strive to maintain the status quo. They are very much against any change that would threaten the relatively secure position they presently occupy. They prefer to be told exactly what to do so that they will not be blamed for any possible mix-up. Conservers supervise their subordinates closely in order to prevent innovation that might upset standardized and tried procedures and policies. In short, you may recognize the conserver as the typical bureaucrat.

The "zealot" is very stubborn and believes he or she knows what is wrong with, or what is best for, the agency or one of its client populations. Win or lose, they fight the good fight, always on the side of right. Typically, zealots have a high energy level. The ability to fight all odds continuously and still maintain enthusiasm is precisely their strength. For these reasons, zealots become excellent change agents. They are often effective in the start-up of a new program or a new agency. Unfortunately, the same degree of innovation is not expected of subordinates. Loyalty to the zealot is.

The "advocate" is a person who has exceptionally high commitment to the goals of the organization or department of which she or he is a member or to a client population serviced by the agency. Great pride is taken in the accomplishment of the agency's or department's service goals. The organization advocate has two major skills: the ability to protect his or her part of the organization against all external threats— hence in a budget meeting, for example, he or she will fight to get the most for her or his agency; and the ability to mediate conflict within his or her department or organization. The combination of these two skills makes the agency advocate the person likely to be promoted to the head of an organization. The client or consumer advocate does the same for those with whom he or she is concerned. In doing so, consumer or client advocates are more likely to be in conflict with others in the agency. Consumer advocates are not as likely to head a service agency as are agency advocates.

All advocates use what can be called a situational approach to leadership. Hence, innovation is encouraged when appropriate and discouraged when superfluous.

The "statesman" tends to be more concerned with the welfare of society as a whole than with the agency or a particular client population. Regardless of the impact on the organization, the statesman will do what he or she *perceives* to be in the best interests of society. Unlikely to devote much time to performing detailed, day-to-day activities, the statesman spends a good deal of time developing overall plans and objectives. Statesmen do well in public relations type situations or any area that interfaces with clients or the public at large. When backed up by managerial staff who are zealots or advocates, they make good agency administrators, but not when left on their own.

Use the exercise that follows to explore how these five concepts might be used in the analysis of your own social agency.

EXERCISE

Describe some of the key persons in your agency with one or more of these characterizations. Do some people fit more than one characterization? Have some moved from being zealots or climbers to conservers as they have stayed in a particular job for a long time? What does that suggest about your agency's personnel policies and practices? Your own career options?

Although we have barely scratched the surface of your agency, we have begun to use one perspective or viewpoint to understand it as an arena for working out career styles and opportunities.

WHERE DOES THIS PERSPECTIVE LEAD YOU?

If you hold the perspective that the agency is indeed an arena within which people respond to change in different ways, and within that arena different styles of managing one's career are possible, then among other things you might:

— pick an agency or work setting in which your own capacities and interests fit the job requirements;

— look for a closeness of fit between the organization and your professional commitments and aspirations;

— select persons for staff positions whose personalities and leadership styles are consistent with those required by the organization to help fulfill its goals;

— define duties and responsibilities of the job to fit the needs, skills, leadership styles, and characteristics of the person selected for the organization;

— deal with interpersonal conflicts or on-the-job problems by accounting for the attitudes, styles, or characteristics of the people involved;

— dismiss an individual who isn't helping to reach the goals of the organization after attempts to relocate her or him to a position more compatible with her or his skills, personality, and other characteristics;

— conclude that reasons for activities not being properly performed involve the lack of feedback and understanding of exactly what is expected rather than that the individual is not motivated or needs training;

— promote a person to a position of more responsibility because she or he is really effective in her or his current job and you see her or him as a competent, capable person in the next level job; and perhaps most important,

— learn as much as possible about the personal leadership styles and personalities of staff members in your own and other key organizations.

STRENGTHS AND LIMITS
OF USING THIS PERSPECTIVE

Strengths	Limits
Personnel practices and job assignments can be designed to encourage change or promote stability.	Every problem may be analyzed only in terms of change and stability. It puts a premium on change.
It can help you find those people for whom change is beneficial and identify those who may be threatened by it.	There is a danger of "psychologizing" every problem and seeing them as the outgrowth of personality types.
Implications of strategies for change within and interaction between organizations can be predicted and analyzed by understanding the people and how they are likely to act in the proposed situation.	It does not do much to clarify roles and responsibilities.
	Approaches to group leadership and efforts of coordination may be ignored because of exclusive focus on individuals—and careers.

Chapter 2

YOUR AGENCY AS A SYSTEM OF ROLES

Just as people can shape organizations, organizations can shape the people within them by requiring that they perform specified roles. Persons assigned to these roles are expected to perform organizational tasks that are considered appropriate to the assigned roles. The distribution of tasks to people in different roles is often reflected in an official job description. But no job description is ever comprehensive or fully accurate. No organization could operate effectively if people did *only* what was contained within their job description, nor could staff members operate effectively if they tried to do everything contained in the usual job description.

PERFORMING ORGANIZATIONAL ROLES

In a given hospital setting, for example, nurses may not be expected to give blood transfusions or to remove stitches from an incision. But in an emergency situation it may be necessary for them to perform one or both of these operations. Over time these tasks may be routinely assigned to one or more nurses but not appear in the formal job description until years later. In a vocational rehabilitation agency, all

37

rehab counselors may be expected to do job counseling, case management, job finding, and job placement with clients of all types and with all kinds of disabilities. In practice, however, staff members in a district office "specialize." One focuses more heavily on working with sight and hearing disabled. Another works with paraplegics. One staff member becomes expert in job finding and job placement, especially in industrial settings. Each performs a somewhat specialized role in relation to his or her co-workers. This role consists in part of the functions, tasks, and activities prescribed by the organization. It also includes tasks undertaken by the role occupant on his or her own initiative or influenced by the expectations held about that role by people who interact with the role occupant.

Some of the people who interact with a role occupant are intended by the ogranization to do so. Examples include superiors, subordinates, and those with whom the person must regularly interact in the performance of his or her assigned tasks. Co-workers can pressure a role occupant to conform to their expectations. Other individuals may have influence because they are important to the role occupant who looks up to them, respects their judgment, and values their approval. These people may occupy positions either within or outside the organization.

A person's own perceptions and interpretations of what is expected for effective role performance also impacts on behavior. All efforts by others to communicate role expectations to a role occupant are subject to interpretation by that person. This filtering process distorts to varying degrees the messages sent to the individual. For example, a supervisor tells a staff member to a call a client who has an emergency. It is almost five o'clock, agency closing time. After about 60 minutes of trying, the staff member reaches the client and offers help. But the supervisor intended the call to be made during office hours. She feels it is unprofessional to call after hours and would generate inappropriate expectations in the future. The staff member is at a loss. "I'm not going all out for clients, if it gets me into trouble," he concludes. "Next time, I'll just follow the rules. The hell with the client." What he did not understand is that the supervisor also was concerned about the client, but she had a different idea about how the professional helping role should be performed.

ROLE/ROLE-SET RELATIONSHIPS

All those people who have influence over someone's role behavior and who interact with the role occupant comprise a "role set." This is the set of other role performers with whom a role occupant interacts. Each of these role performers interacts with others in their role sets. That is why we call it a system of roles. The role set can become an extremely important unit of analysis in trying to understand role performance. Sources of interpersonal conflict are often found in role performance-role set interactions. It is sometimes more effective to try to influence someone indirectly through his or her role set than by approaching the person directly. Solutions to job performance problems can often be found in role-role set interactions.

Whatever the nature of the interactions, many roles endure over time, regardless of their occupants or others in the role set. The job of typist, for example, exists beyond the life of the role occupant. This is a major stabilizing factor for the organization. Although each occupant modifies the role performed, a substantial portion of the role often remains unchanged regardless of who occupies the role. Some observers feel that when someone new is placed into an existing role, he or she is more likely to act very similarly to the person who previously held that role, rather than to the way he or she acted in a previous role. Others expect it, and one comes to respond to those expectations. Somehow the role and other people's expectations of the role require people to behave in ways consistent with past role behavior. Nevertheless, individuals do perform a particular role differently from others in that role. To understand this point, think about actors in a play. Roles are generally established and defined in the script. But different actors will bring different styles, interpretations, and experiences to the same role. The role will never be portrayed by two performers in exactly the same way. What one actor does with a role may also be affected by how other actors play their roles or how the director wants the script interpreted. Nevertheless, the role continues to exist beyond the life of any particular player.

Consider a staff role previously occupied by a person who did everything he or she was told, but no more. Assume that a new person now occupies this same role who has a lot of energy and is willing to do whatever will help the agency. The new person is intelligent and wants to learn. In time the expectations of people for his or her role performance will differ from what they were for the first person in this role. The basic job description has remained the same, but the expected role behavior is substantially changed.

EXPECTATIONS, CONFLICTS, AND STRAINS

If everyone in organizations both understood and sent complementary role messages, lived up to role expectations, and made compatible role demands,there would be few problems in interpersonal and organizational behavior. Unfortunately, things don't happen that way. Problems in the performance of roles can and do occur.

Role conflict occurs when contradictory expectations exist for role performance and living up to one expectation makes compliance with another difficult, if not impossible. *Role strain* is the discomfort experienced when role conflict is encountered. Role conflict can usually be identified by examining the expectations held by the person and members of his or her role set. There are a number of possible sources for role conflict. Individuals can and do occupy more than one role at a time, and different roles may not always be compatible. For example, being supervisor of some staff and subordinate of others are incompatible roles for some people. Sources of conflict include "double messages," contradictory signals from two senders; lack of knowledge, skill, or resources to fill a role; lack of clarity about expected behavior; lack of time or energy to perform; and conflicts emerging from the role occupant's personality traits that are out of synch with required behaviors.

Some observers suggest that persons occupying certain kinds of roles in organizations are especially likely to experience role strain and conflict. They tend to be (1) those in contact with the external environment who must satisfy expectations of both people within the organization and people outside of it; (2) those expected to provide innovative ideas that may not set well with colleagues and supervisors; and (3) those in middle management positions who must respond to both supervisors and subordinates.

Role strain is often associated with job stress and burnout. The symptoms associated with burnout are by now well known. They include loss of interest in work or in the service mission of the agency; "work-to-rule" (that is, doing just enough to get by, or following agency procedures to the letter even when flexibility based on professional judgment would be more appropriate); performing one's role in such a way as to disassociate one's self personally from it—making no real investment in the role.

Understanding the position and the accompanying roles that individuals hold can provide insight into organizational behavior. Role analysis can aid in planning more effective divisions of labor and in solving problems that seem not to get resolved at the interpersonal level. It also provides new ideas for alternative solutions of implementing change. The following exercise should illustrate the point. It is intended to help people who interact with one another compare *what is happening* with *what they would like to see happening*. While it is a fairly straightforward exercise, it often reveals interesting discrepancies. Ideally, it should be worked through in a nonthreatening situation with a wide range of staff.

— Bring together key persons who have contact with one another.

— Ask each person to list the tasks he or she performs on the job.

— Have each person list the behaviors he or she feels are expected of him or her by two significant other persons in the room.

— Have each person also list the behaviors he or she expects of two other persons in the group.

— Use the chart below to help order your statements.

ROLE TITLE

Persons with whom I have contact	What I think they expect from me	What I expect of myself
1. _____	_____	_____
_____	_____	_____
_____	_____	_____
_____	_____	_____
2. _____	_____	_____
_____	_____	_____
_____	_____	_____
_____	_____	_____
3. _____	_____	_____
_____	_____	_____
_____	_____	_____
_____	_____	_____
4. _____	_____	_____
_____	_____	_____
_____	_____	_____
_____	_____	_____
5. _____	_____	_____
_____	_____	_____
_____	_____	_____
_____	_____	_____

Be very specific. List behaviors, not feelings. If feelings are part of the expectations, include the behaviors that are used to evidence the feelings.

— Now exchange this chart with the persons on your list. Ask them to star the statements that differ from their own perceptions.

— Compare lists. Check perceived messages against the messages on the charts. Pay attention to discrepancies, conflicts, and inaccurate statements.

— Consider what strategies could be used to bring inconsistent statements together. This may include rewriting job descriptions, restructuring supervisor lines, reassigning certain tasks, or clarifying communication.

WHERE DOES THIS PERSPECTIVE LEAD YOU?

Among other things, if you hold the perspective that organizations are systems of roles, you might

— want to design clear, written job descriptions, with performance criteria so that everyone knows what is to be expected of the role occupant;

— try to avoid unclear or competing expectations that make it difficult for staff members to perform their jobs;

— establish an ongoing mechanism for clarification and evaluation of role expectations and demands, for both new and experienced workers;

— avoid spending excessive time resolving role problems rather than doing organizational problem solving or improving service delivery;

STRENGTHS AND LIMITS
OF USING THIS PERSPECTIVE

Strengths	Limits
Positions can be initially defined so that they are not dependent on the people who fill them. Activities or tasks required in a role can be explained to others.	It may lead to a static conception of jobs and positions. Positions tend to perpetuate themselves. Organizational interaction may be portrayed as a series of faulty messages and unclear expectations rather than examining the larger organizational picture.
Attention to the above can assure that the next occupant in the position has fewer problems in understanding his or her job.	Organizational structures and the intended interaction patterns are not adequately distinguished.
Blaming people for individual behaviors is deemphasized through understanding of the attributes required for effective performance.	
Key People who occupy any role or people who occupy key roles can be analyzed in terms of their role sets to monitor role performance and possible reasons for inadequate role behavior.	
The organization can change even when the roles remain the same. As different people occupy a role, the role set changes—thereby increasing opportunities for change.	

Chapter 3

YOUR AGENCY AS A SYSTEM OF SMALL GROUPS

Organizations of all sizes can be viewed as systems of small groups. The emergence of both formal work groups and informal social groups is inevitable. It occurs throughout every organization. Groups mobilize powerful forces that have strong effects on the individual. From the organization's point of view, these effects may be good in that they help fulfill the goals of the organization or bad in that they hinder organizational goal attainment. The more you understand about the dynamics of behavior, the more likely you will be able to use these dynamics for the good of the organization.

GROUP NORMS

Before moving on, we want to discuss the emergence of group norms. A norm is a standard of behavior that is accepted and legitimated by members of a group. Norms exist for all groups and are a controlling influence on the attitudes and behaviors of group members. They evolve over time and emerge from the interactions of group members.

Norms may be formal and explicit or informal but understood by everyone who has been a group member for a reasonable length of time. For example, it may be a norm in one agency that staff members behave with restraint in monthly staff meetings; at another agency, that they take this opportunity to confront agency administration. In most cases, members of a group who do not follow established norms will feel pressure from other group members to conform. This is true regardless of whether membership in the group is voluntary or involuntary. Adherence to the norms of the group is a requirement for acceptance by others. Some people may feel less pressured to conform to group norms. The marginal member has, by definition, few ties to the group. For different reasons, the informal leader and much sought-after members may also be able to deviate from the norms. Their prestige makes it possible for them to break the rules or establish new ones.

INFLUENCING LEADERS

Because group leaders often epitomize the norms of a group, it pays to find out who plays a leadership role in each group with which you are concerned. By understanding how and why the group's leader(s) acts as he or she does, you may learn a good deal about the group's interactions with other groups, with a supervisor, or with client populations. Norms influence the way in which members of the group behave. The group's leader has the highest potential influence on the norms of the group and thus on the behavior of its members. It follows that if you want to influence the group informally, you should direct your efforts at the group leader who in turn can modify the norms and behavior of all or most of the group members.

But trying to influence the group leader is only part of the picture. Leaders are not very influential in groups that don't stick together very well. The same is true of group norms. Norms are powerful controls on member behavior. By group cohesion, I mean the extent to which group members are attracted to the group and feel a part of it. The stronger this attraction, the more effective the group norms are in influencing the behavior of a particular member. In a highly cohesive group, the leader may be able to more strongly influence, or perhaps control, the behavior of the members. This increases the importance of influencing the group leader if you want to induce the group to change its collective behavior.

THE FUNCTIONS OF INFORMAL GROUPS

I mentioned earlier that the formation of informal groups is inevitable in an organization, but I did not explain why this is so. Isn't the pressure to conform to group norms too great a cost to the individual? If so, why identify with the group? We all give up some of our individuality when we become group members, but we also gain something in terms of personal identity and effectiveness. If there were no benefits derived from membership there would be no motivation to join. There are at least three major benefits to informal group membership: established identity; increased task accomplishment; and emotional support. Joining a group gives one a sense of shared identity. Being a member of a group that has high status results in transfer of that status to the group's members.

A second reason for joining a group relates to task completion. Often a group can give needed assistance in meeting individual goals and completing a job that the individual could not do alone. For example, when assisting a client, a staff member may need the knowledge and expertise held by another group member. Being a member of a group increases the likelihood that needed information will be more readily available. Other staff members are willing to help since they know that they can call on this member to reciprocate and help with their clients in the future.

Finally, a group gives emotional support to its members. One can let one's hair down in one's group, blow off steam, and share one's frustrations with people who are expected to understand and be supportive. This emotional support makes the work place more gratifying and satisfying. But some groups don't work well. They may not be supportive of individual members. Some groups operate to frustrate the aims of the overall organization. Their norms may be incompatible with the purposes of the agency. This, of course, is not necessarily bad. It can serve to force others within the organization to examine its purposes, its priorities, and its programs.

One more point: Groups tend to make more extreme decisions than individuals. It is easier to take a risk in a group, particularly when there is a strong leader in the group or when consensus is strong, than when one is totally and individually responsible for a decision. Union actions are good examples. Individual risks are reduced in proportion to the cohesiveness of "solidarity" of union members. However, groups that are not cohesive, that are little more than time-limited collections of individuals (like some committees), are not likely to take risks. They tend to settle for those actions that are least likely to "rock the boat."

There are important implications for your agency in this phenomenon. For example, a manager may not want to or may be incapable of making a decision and therefore will delegate his responsibility. While the manager cannot control the *specific* decision to be made, he or she *can* influence the amount of risk that will be taken in that decision. If a very high risk or low risk decision is desired, the decision should be delegated to the appropriate group. Should a more moderate decision be desired, this activity is best delegated to an individual or less cohesive group.

EXERCISE

Before you go on, describe two situations on separate sheets of paper: one in which you belonged to a cohesive group and one in which the group was only minimally connected interpersonally. For each, answer the following questions.

1. Can you recall a situation in which the group attempted to pressure you and behave in some way that you felt conflicted with your own values? Describe.

2. How did you react? Describe.

3. What was the outcome of your reaction and the group pressure? Describe.

4. Based on the foregoing discussion, what might you do to make certain that neither you nor others will be put in such a position again?

WHERE DOES THIS PERSPECTIVE LEAD YOU?

Among other things, if you hold the perspective that organizations are systems of small groups you might:

— use group norms rather than administrative mandate to facilitate change or further accomplishment of the organization's aims;

— isolate individuals or groups, or remove individuals from groups whose norms do not adhere to organizational norms to improve administrative control;

— hire individuals whose values are consistent with organizatinal norms to ensure smooth staff interaction;

— keep groups small enough and with people of similar backgrounds to increase cohesion in groups that help attain organizational goals;

— encourage diversity among group norms in the interest of promoting organizational change;

— include group leaders in staff meetings that may affect the norms of the group to aid in increasing acceptance of change by group members;

— emphasize similarities of community and organizational norms to promote community support;

— decide the degree of risk desired to determine whether decisions should be made by individuals or groups.

STRENGTHS AND LIMITS OF USING THIS PERSPECTIVE

Strengths	Limits
The organization can be perceived as being composed of informal groups, each with a life of its own and each with interests that influence organizational effectiveness.	This approach emphasizes what happens to small groups rather than the organization as a whole and to its service goals.
Various groups within the organization can be mobilized to contribute to the total organization.	It does not give enough attention to formal organizational structure or lines of authority.
Change within the organization can be encouraged by building on divergent group norms.	It emphasizes the process of interpersonal interaction rather than the results of service delivery.
Individuals can find support in groups whose norms are most similar or acceptable to their own.	An inappropriate focus on group norms may result in pressures toward conformity.

Strengths	Limits
The organization can find and retain individuals whose personal values are similar to its norms.	Inappropriate emphasis on improving group cohesion can eliminate the potential gains derived from individual innovation.
The riskiness of decisions can be influenced even if the content of a decision cannot be controlled.	
Acceptance of change can be enhanced by including at least the group leaders in the decision-making process.	
Leaders can be encouraged to help influence the direction group norms take and, therefore, group members behavior.	

Chapter 4

YOUR AGENCY AS A FORMAL ORGANIZATION

The most common way to represent an organization's formal structure is by drawing an organization chart. Organization charts show the formal division of work within an organization. They are composed of boxes and lines between them, each box representing a work unit (a position or department). The lines between boxes designate the lines of authority or communication connecting them. Authority lines depict who is directly responsible to whom; communication lines depict the flow of information through formal communication channels. This may include the directives that are sent down from management and upward reporting from lower work units. Superior-subordinate positions are shown in terms of organizational levels. Organization charts (sometimes called "organigrams") can also be used to show each work unit's function within the larger organization. It may be easier to understand this by seeing it. Look at the two relatively typical organization charts that follow.

ORGANIZATION CHARTS

In Chart 1 the relationships between several units in a mental health clinic are shown: accounting, intake, treatment (counseling), staff development, and research and development. Only four levels of hierarchical relationships are shown. If we were to assume that the clinic is part of a larger organization, say a regional mental hospital, the clinic might have been shown as only one of several clinics, all part of a community mental health center serving a subregion under the jurisdiction of the hospital. Thus the chart would have included at least two additional levels.

The chart depicts only the formal dimensions of the hierarchical relationships. It gives no information about what happens within a work unit (role-related and normative behavior). Positions or offices are the unit of analysis, and only the formal relationships between positions are shown. Yet these relationships help to examine issues of interdependence, locate points of potential conflict, and permit examination of direction of work and communication flow.

Moreover, the specific way the total organization is set up—for example, how many subordinates each supervisor has directly under his or her control—can tell you a great deal about the agency. Two agencies with exactly the same number of employees might be structured very differently. The first may have a relatively small number of subordinates for each supervisor and, therefore a large number of layers or levels. This increases the chances for red tape. Since communication lines are long, this agency is somewhat inflexible to change because it takes so long for information to get up to the top and directives to get back down. It is likely that supervision will be close since there are fewer subordinates.

Chart 2 depicts a second agency, one with a large number of subordinates for every supervisor but a small number of hierarchical levels. The chances are that this agency can react and adapt quickly to change because communication lines

Chart 1

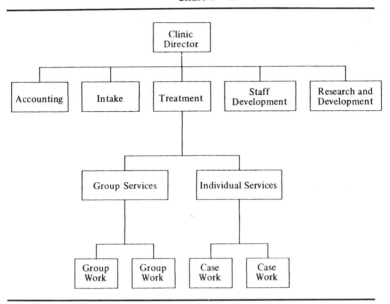

are short. This might mean that as the needs of clients shift and as interactions with other agencies change, the second agency can handle its new situation more flexibly than the first one we examined. Moreover, because there are so many employees, each supervisor will probably delegate responsibility to lower level employees.

Its formal leadership style is likely to be different than that found in the first agency. Unlike the agency in Chart 1, this agency may face a coordination problem. It is generally easier to coordinate the efforts of many units or individuals when you have a tall structure with reverse hierarchical levels, rather than a flat structure where authority is diffused across fewer levels. It may be necessary to employ experts for the coordination effort. This effort may require management training experts rather than those with expertise in a particular field of practice such as family treatment or psychiatric nursing.

Chart 2

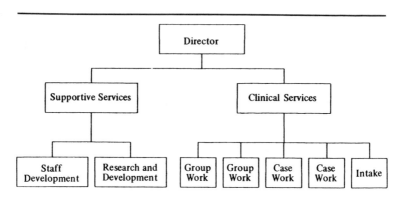

Chart 3 illustrates how the organization chart can be used to map the relationship between work groups. It is a somewhat different way of depicting what we showed on Chart 1. Every position, with the exception of the very top and very bottom ones, belongs to two work groups. By taking the first organization chart shown above and superimposing the work group triangles, we see a different picture of the communication across organizational levels. The Supervisor for Group Services, for example, is depicted as superior to the staff in the Group Work units. As such he or she hands down the policies sent from above. But this supervisor is also a subordinate to the person responsible for treatment. This provides the supervisor an opportunity to send up to his or her supervisor the views of the group workers. And the person responsible for the treatment program can, as a subordinate to the Clinic Director, pass these views to the top. Depicting the formal structure of your agency this way helps you understand how work groups can be used to facilitate communication both

Chart 3

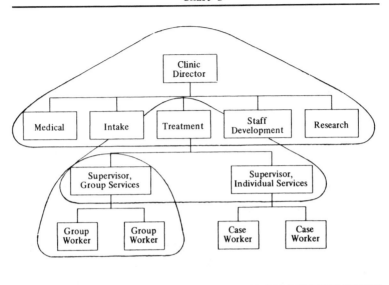

up and down, how agency activities can be coordinated, and which units should be located within a larger substructure of the whole agency. The organization chart is basically a map that describes formal relationships within an organization. Some people don't like to use them, arguing that no map can tell you everything about an organization. They point out that charts don't show the "real" organization which they define as made up of informal relationships and procedures that emerge as people go about performing the tasks required on the job. While it is true that the informal organization is not *directly* dealt with when one looks at the formal structure, this perspective does open up a rich source of information and suggests alternative ways of solving organization problems and those identified in the preceding chapters.

DESIGNING ORGANIZATION CHARTS

Before we go on to examine the strengths and limits of this perspective, we would like you to design two organization charts for your agency. Follow the instructions below or modify them to be more useful to you.

EXERCISE 1: FORMAL ORGANIZATION CHART

— If a formal organization chart exists for your agency, haul it out and look it over.

— Does it fit what you know to be true about the present structure of your organization? If yes, go on to Exercise 2.

— If there is no organization chart, or if the chart is outdated, gather information to make a current chart. You will probably find that you have more information than you can fit onto a formal organization chart.

EXERCISE 2: INFORMAL ORGANIZATION CHART

— Put aside the formal organization chart.

— Think about who talks to whom in the agency. Think about to whom you go for important information about your job. With whom do you ride to work or eat lunch?

— Observe the same process in your supervisor, your coworker, and an agency administrator.

— Make a chart of what you think is the informal organization. Draw lines of communication, of formal authority, and of the power relationships between people or work units.

— Place yourself somewhere on the chart. With whom do you most often interact? Around what issues?

EXERCISE 3: IDENTIFYING CRITICAL LOCATIONS

— Locate and mark the decision makers in your organization on both charts.

— First indicate those with formal authority in one color of ink. Then locate the informal leaders, including gatekeepers (for example, phone receptionists, secretaries, intake workers) in a second color.

This exercise should help you visualize much of what goes on in the agency in which you work. A lot of information simply will not fit on any chart. This is one of the reasons charts are limited in their utility. On the other hand, they are graphic depictions of data that are often obscured or forgotten.

WHERE DOES THIS PERSPECTIVE LEAD YOU?

If you view an agency as a system of formal structures, you might:

— draw an organization chart to trace the formal lines of communication between work units;

— problem solve along structural lines, for example, change the location of a supervisor, or change the number of units supervised or numbers of organizational layers, rather than focus on personal issues;

— locate all work groups within the organizational map and understand how they all interrelate;

— describe the type of organization structure you have and the advantages and disadvantages of it.

STRENGTHS AND LIMITS
OF USING THIS PERSPECTIVE

Strengths	Limits
It makes the formal lines of authority and the division of labor explicit, making it easier to know when and if changes should be made.	Too much focus on the formal structure without recognition of informal relationships presents an incomplete view of the organization.
It makes possible the identification of places where formal structures can be changed to more closely coincide with informal interaction patterns.	Looking at structures sometimes results in a static view of the organization—it is a snapshot—it freezes the action while losing sight of the interactions between units and within them.
Organizations make it possible to depict the flow of authority and information within an organization and to communicate these simply and directly to others.	The human dimension is largely excluded from view.

Chapter 5

YOUR AGENCY AS AN INPUT-OUTPUT PROCESSING SYSTEM

Until now, we've examined your agency as if it had no business; that is, as if it did not do anything for or on behalf of others. Were we to end our analysis at this point, it would leave us with only fragmentary perspectives of the whole. In the discussion that follows we will examine the agency from a structure-functional perspective; that is, we will look at those subsystems of the whole that make it possible for the agency to get the resources it needs and to transform them into products for distribution.[1]

FUNCTIONAL SUBSYSTEMS AND THEIR INTERRELATIONSHIPS

Every social agency is composed of a set of interrelated units or subsystems designed to achieve a common set of objectives. The activities of these units are aimed at (1) *recruiting inputs* into the agency, such as money, credit, clients, and staff; (2) *processing inputs,* or changing them from money, credit, clients, staff, and other inputs into such programs and

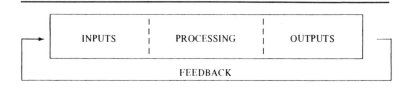

Figure 1

services as prevention, education, counseling, rehabilitation, or day treatment; and (3) *producing outputs,* such as healthier people or improved education in the schools. For systems to survive or to maintain themselves, they must take in at least as many resources as they consume. To maintain itself, your agency must divert some of the resources that could be used for production into maintenance activities. Therefore, *more* inputs are required than those used for outputs.

In every system output has a return effect (feedback) on the resources that enter and re-enter the agency. The types of outputs—for example, workshops conducted, or reduction in number of students addicted to drugs in the local high school—influence the amount of money, types of clients, and other resources that flow into the system. The process can be charted as shown in Figure 1.

Within the larger system, four major subsystems can be identified. Each performs a specific function, without which the agency will experience difficulties. Actors involved in one particular subsystem have a common kind of motivation. In small agencies, one person may work in several or all subsystems. However, work within each subsystem usually requires specific motivation, knowledge, and skills appropriate to that subsystem. Although the four subsystems will be presented separately, in the real world they exist in a state of ongoing interaction. A change in one subsystem will have an impact on the other three and the entire organization.

The four subsystems perform the following functions: (1) production; (2) boundary exchange; (3) adaptation and (4) management. These are diagrammed in Figure 2.

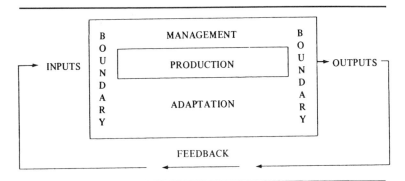

Figure 2

The Production Subsystem. In a human service agency the function of the production subsystem is to provide service.[2] Resources (inputs) such as money and manpower entering the agency are transformed into services. The importance of this subsystem is demonstrated by the fact that the agency's name or its classification is often related to the service it provides. An example of this is a "child guidance clinic." If we diagrammed only the productions subsystem, it would look as in Figure 3.

The Boundary Subsystem. Like all organizations, human service agencies rely on imputs from their environment for survival, and they produce outputs to that environment. The function of the boundary subsystem is to obtain from the environment those resources needed to perform the tasks of the production subsystem and to return the "products" or services to the environment. Resources processed by the boundary subsystem include:

— money and credit to cover costs of both providing services and maintaining the agency;

— personnel such as administrators, counselors, doctors, nurses, clerical staff and others;

— clients;

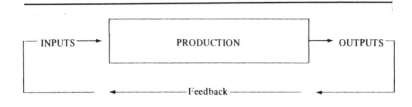

Figure 3

— knowledge and expertise to implement services;

— complementary services from other agencies;

— social support and legitimation from the environment such as other service agencies, potential clients, community influentials, regulatory agencies, and so on.

Accounting for both the production and boundary subsystems, the agency diagram has grown to look like Figure 4. Staff performing boundary functions are faced with competing expectations—those of members of their role sets within their own organizations and those of others who comprise external role sets. A crisis center director, for example, might experience conflicting demands from agency staff who want to protect the privacy of juvenile runaways and from the police who want to follow the letter of the law. When agency staff perform "outward facing" activities such as recruiting volunteers, going after funding, or working as outreach workers to contact potential clients, they are performing boundary functions. Staff activities to develop ties with community influentials, improve public relations, or place recovered clients in half-way houses are other examples of boundary functions.

The Adaptive Subsystem. The adaptive subsystem permits the agency to modify its activities in regard to a changing environment. In part, it performs an intelligence function, evaluating the activities of the agency in relation to changes in that environment. An agency that cannot adapt to new client needs, new state requirements, or funding priorities quickly becomes obsolete. Obsolete agencies find it difficult to recruit

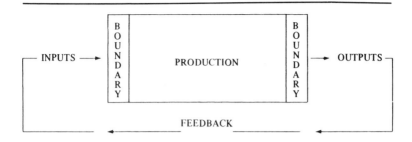

Figure 4

resources, including clients and the money and manpower to serve them. When you add the adaptive subsystem to the other two, the agency diagram looks like Figure 5.

The three functions of the adaptive subsystem are to

— audit the external environment of the agency;

— monitor internal activities; and

— evaluate outputs.

Auditing the external environment requires being alert to changes in units upon which the agency is dependent (e.g., a state office, a local board, funders, etc.). It also involves identifying developments in service technology (e.g., new forms of therapy, new management techniques) that might supersede or replace those employed by the agency. Finally, it involves assessing changes in client needs or populations. For example, the increased use of alcohol by secondary school children might suggest new client populations in need of treatment by agency staff.

External auditing requires that those agency people who "face outward"—the directors, board chairpersons, and program developers—keep abreast of environmental changes. These include changes in both available resources and the suppliers of resources. Those persons managing the adaptive subsystem

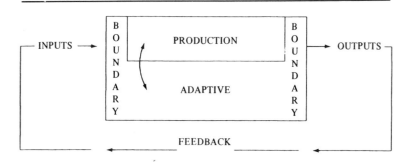

Figure 5

of resources. Those persons managing the adaptive subsystem must possess analytic skills to assess and evaluate changes in the environment and interactional skills to negotiate effectively with elements in the environment. Monitoring internal activities requires collecting information at two levels: the "client level" and the "operations level." Client level information includes client perceptions of needs, worker perceptions of client needs, and actions taken by the agency regarding the client. It is a record keeping function that ensures more rational and continuous client service, and provides data for a more comprehensive look at an agency's clients.

Auditing at the "operations level" involves gathering and analyzing information about recruiting clients to the agency; the kinds of services offered to different types of clients; staff case loads; and kinds of interventions used. These records deal with ongoing aspects of agency performance and provide information about agency operations.

Evaluation of agency outputs is often a legal or fiscal requirement, particularly when the agency has to justify its existence and the continuation of its services. Evaluation also informs agency staff and others of the effectiveness of their efforts. Few evaluations are easy to conduct. Valid measures are difficult to arrive at. The results of an evaluation may be painful. Evaluations are complicated by the fact that most

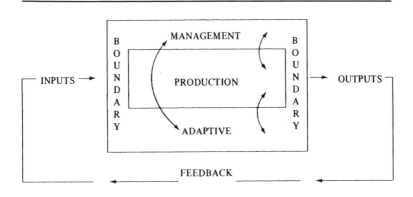

Figure 6

agencies have multiple goals that result in multiple outputs. For these reasons agencies often short-circuit the evaluation process or avoid it. This is unfortunate because without adequate evaluation, feedback is incomplete and the agency is less likely to be able to adjust effectively to environmental changes.

The Management Subsystem. Cutting across all others, the management subsystem's activities include coordinating the activities of staff performing in each subsystem; resolving conflicts among the subsystems and the organizational hierarchy to maintain adequate staff performance; and mediating the demands of the internal and external systems. It is at this level that goals and priorities are set and guidelines for the organization are designed. The final agency diagram looks like Figure 6.

Note that Figure 6 does not quite correspond to the formal organization discussed in Chapter 4. In fact, while different functions tend to be allocated to different work units, any work unit within a complex organization might perform all or part of the functions associated with the four subsystems.

Managers must understand the functions of all four subsystems if they are to effectively coordinate those functions and resolve conflicts. Just as the total system has two motivations—survival and service—so does each subsystem. Managers make decisions about allocating resources between those conflicting motivations. The primary function of the managerial subsystem is to maintain the organization. By so doing it provides support for the other subsystems. Managerial decisions often represent compromises between members of various subsystems. If those compromises respond only to the most strident voices, they may lead to inconsistent or unworkable agency policies. A good administrator must be able to make tolerable compromises, compromises that assure effective agency operation. This approach differs from more traditional views of management in which administrators direct, staff perform tasks, and administrators check to see if directives were fulfilled. It leads to negotiations and shared decision making in management.

EXAMPLES OF THE SYSTEMS APPROACH

The preceding discussion summarized what is often referred to as *the* "systems approach" and draws on the work of sociologist Talcott Parsons. It would be better to refer to it as *a* systems approach, because Parson's work has been complemented by the contributions of other theorists. Whatever we choose to call it, we might all agree that the systems perspective requires management to perform flexibly. If the manager recognizes the organization's multiple and often incompatible goals, his or her trust will be toward workable compromise in the face of incompatible demands. Managers should be seen as persons who explore organizational resources and seek modification rather than establishing and enforcing hard and fast rules. The systems approach to management goes beyond reacting to what is, in order to project what might be or should be. It requires the manager to explore alternative means of using inputs to achieve outputs. It suggests the need to define and redefine those outputs in terms of organizational goals. Figure 7 summarizes the preceding discussion. The following exercises will help you think through the information you have read about agency subsystems. Use them or other examples drawn from your own experience to help colleagues understand how to approach organizational problems and operations from the systems perspective.

EXERCISE A

The child placement agency never seems to find out about changes in state and federal regulations until the last minute. It is constantly struggling to make last minute adjustments in its programs and apply for new licenses.

In what subsystems is the problem located? How will it affect the other subsystems?

In this example, the problem lies in the adaptive subsystem—in the failure of those doing the auditing to be alert to the changes indicated by state and federal regulating agencies. It is not enough to be in contact with state and federal officials. It may also be necessary to be ready to shift agency operations in the direction of the general policy drift. Your organization must be willing to assign adequate resources to both auditing and in preparation for possible adaptation. To survive, it may be necessary to anticipate changes and be ready to adapt rapidly.

Inefficiency in this subsystem affects each of the other subsystems. The effect on other subsystems would depend upon what state or federal regulation changes occur. For example, if new regulations concern staff training, the managerial subsystem and the boundary subsystem are most affected. The boundary subsystem has to secure the resources from the environment such as trainers and facilities in order to provide the new training. The managerial subsystem then has to coor-

Production Subsystem

Function: — accomplishment of work
related tasks

— transformation of energy
within agency

Motivation: effectiveness and efficiency in service delivery

Boundary Subsystem

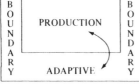

Function: — management of exchanges
at system boundaries to
obtain resources

— maintenance and recruitment of social support

Motivation: acquisition of needed
inputs and assurance of
market for outputs

Adaptive Subsystem

Function: — assessment of needs

— feedback and evaluation

Motivation: response to pressure for
change or exploration of
new opportunities for
service

Management Subsystem

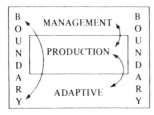

Function: — coordination and direction of substructures

— support of staff in adequate job performance

— coordination of external
demands and agency
resources;

— maintenance of organizational activities

Motivation: maintenance or expansion
of production, adaptive
and boundary subsystems

Figure 7 Summary of Agency Subsystems

dinate the activities of staff while they undergo the training to meet regulations. The production subsystem is affected as staff are required to reallocate their time from direct services to training.

Now consider another example, Exercise B.

EXERCISE B

Agency Y has been unsuccessful in its attempts to initiate an alcohol safety court referral program in its county. The adjacent two counties have had such programs for over a year. Every time the director proposes that the County Board of Commissioners consider his proposal, the idea is supported but the program never has gotten beyond the expression of support stage. The director seems unable to get actual budgeting for the program and has been unable to enlist the aid of any single member of the Board.

In which subsystem is the problem located?
Which subsystem could bring pressure to bear on the Board?
Which combination of could be used to solve this problem?

Work out the answers yourself or with your agency colleagues.

If you prefer, reflect on an organizational problem you have recently experienced. How did you resolve that problem? In which subsystem did it lie? If the problem still exists, confront it using a systems perspective. Utilize what you have learned about subsystems to locate a point at which problem resolution could be aimed. If you are finding some difficulty in working this problem through, why not work on it at a staff meeting?

WHERE DOES THIS PERSPECTIVE LEAD YOU?

Among other things, if you view the organization as a system of subsystems you might

— develop a picture of your agency operations that extends beyond the individual unit or agency;

— be better able to identify and locate resources you want and need in your service delivery system;

— develop a better understanding of other units both inside and outside your agency or department;

— be able to anticipate potential problems and develop organizational mechanisms to handle risk and uncertainty;

— be able to better balance the resources spent on agency maintenance and services;

— be aware of the interdependencies of all the subsystems and that a change in one subsystem affects all other subsystems.

STRENGTHS AND LIMITS
OF USING THIS PERSPECTIVE

Strengths	Limits
The systems approach encompasses the entire organization—structural subunits, task groups, and individuals.	In focusing on the entire system, the major purpose of the organization—the production function—may be downgraded in importance.
It makes it possible to consider allocation of resources to both agency survival and service delivery more rationally.	
It specifies which functions should be carried out by the appropriate subunits of an organization.	It involves a high initial investment of time and energy to establish the task and performance measures that accompany this approach.
It permits a more rational approach to management of organizations that deal in human problems and often find themselves buried in value-laden issues. It aims toward compromise and negotiation.	It is often difficult for staff to understand this perspective because it may not be a familiar one.
It is an integrative perspective that ties all the subsystems together for a common purpose of organizational goal attainment.	

NOTES

1. The perceptive reader will find that this chapter is based on Talcott Parsons's seminal contributions to sociological literature. See especially Parsons et al. (1961).

2. Some readers might take objection to designating agency output as service. "If the goal of service is some change in the consumer or client, shouldn't that change be designated as the output?" Hold your reservation. We'll deal with this issue in the next chapter.

Chapter 6

YOUR AGENCY IN INTERACTION WITH ITS ENVIRONMENT

The agency's adaptive system, when it is working well, makes it possible to interact with various elements in the environment in a relatively systematic and planned manner. But how does the environment impact on the agency, its ability to survive amidst turbulance, and to accomplish the missions for which it was established? In this chapter we'll examine two sets of concepts that can be used to understand environmental influences and then, based on that understanding, how an agency charts a course through the environment. The first conceptual approach is drawn from biology and is generally referred to as *human ecology*. The second is drawn from social psychology and deals with *agency/organization-set* relationships, which parallel those we discussed in Chapter 2 when we examined role/role-set relationships.

ECOLOGICAL INFLUENCES ON YOUR AGENCY

Ecologists refer to *symbiotic* and *commensalistic* interdependence between organisms and their environments. Symbiosis presumes differences in both characteristics and aims, yet these differences are essential for organisms to interact. Bees in need of nectar and flowers in need of pollination provide a familiar example. In systems terminology we would say that one system's output is another's input. Symbiosis can be used to describe many of the relationships between agencies and within them. Interagency referrals or purchase of service agreements are examples of symbiotic exchanges between organizations. Exchanges between a secretarial pool and the protective services staff in a public welfare agency might serve as an internal example.

In contrast, commensalistic interdependence is based on common characteristics or interests. These are expressed in terms of common behavior and shared goals. A union, a fundraising group, or a child advocacy league are typical examples of commensalistic associations. These are single organizations. For an example of commensalistic cooperation between organizations, consider six child welfare agencies cooperating on a volunteer recruitment or public awareness campaign. The type of cooperation established will generally be the result of a variety of environmental forces impacting on the organism (your agency), but the specific impact those forces have will be mediated by the technology available to and used by the agency. An examination of the mental health system may clarify the point.

The mental hospital in your community can be viewed as the product of centuries of effort to control the threatening behavior of some members of society (referred to as social deviants or defined as mentally ill or incompetent), in such a way as to protect the rest of society. So long as society does not change its perception of the mentally ill, and so long as the technologies used for treatment and control do not change, we would expect that the system would not be subject to pressures to modify its behavior or structure.

As newer technologies were developed, particularly those involving drugs, it was possible to treat patients differently. But so long as the community was not ready to accept the mentally ill within its own midst, or so long as effective methods of community management were not developed, it was not possible to discharge large numbers of patients. Thus, many of the earlier modalities of treatment remain commonplace: physical restraints, shock, involvement of patients in some form of therapeutic work or self-help. To understand this in ecological terms, let's consider the hosptial and its environment as an ecosystem.

All ecosystems tend toward the maintenance of an equilibrium state; that is, without any internal or external pressures, systems will tend to remain in a steady state with no need to change. But if there are pressures to change (say in the form of public protest or through the infusion of new funds to establish a new service), such changes will take place in some part of the system, through modifying the functions of a particular department, enlarging it, or establishing a new program. Once such change has been initiated, there is internal pressure for other departments to change. The system is no longer in a steady state, and to correct for the internal pressures, the organism (mental hospital) tries to make adjustments that will lead it to a new equilibrium.

Ecosystems tend to be relatively permeable or impermeable, or in less technical terms, relatively open or closed. So long as persons defined as mentally ill were committed to mental hospitals and those hospitals provided all needed services to their patients, the system was relatively closed. The hospital depended on the outside primarily for a steady infusion of funds and for the referral or commitment of patients. But when the preferred treatment shifted to community care (based on new public perceptions or definitions of mental illness as mediated by new technology—primarily chemical treatment), mental hospitals found themselves involved in a wide variety of new symbiotic and commensalistic relationships with other organizations. As the hospital's success in rehabilitating patients (not just warehousing them) depended more and more on the availability of community support systems, a larger

number of staff members began to perform boundary functions, interacting with various elements in the community.
Whereas at one time the hospital's superintendent or its medical
director may have had exclusive responsibility for relating to
the environment, now such repsonsibiity is broadly shared.
The sheer number of needed external relationships, their
complexity and variety, require that many members of the
staff develop and maintain relationships with suppliers and
collaborators. Rehabilitation and treatment are no longer possible
within the hospital itself. Often, they require cooperative ar-
rangements with many other social and health agencies. In
ecological terms the hospital has become a relatively open
system, its boundaries increasingly permeable. A better term
might even by "diffuse." The more open an organization
and diffuse its boundaries, the less importance is placed on
those boundaries (where the organization stops and another
one begins), and the more emphasis is placed on improving
the nature of the functional interdependence the organization
has developed with key elements it its environment. It may
even become difficult to tell where one agency ends and another
begins. In community mental health, for example, it is not
uncommon to find consultants and others employed by a mental health center, functioning as staff members of a high school,
senior citizen's center, or city recreation department. Whatever
boundaries might exist must be redrawn continuously if any
organization chart is to remain current.

THE TASK ENVIRONMENT
AND THE ORGANIZATION-SET

Let's now reexamine these same processes using a somewhat
different set of concepts. The entire array of agencies, people,
and groups with which an agency interacts to provide services
and to survive is called a "task environment" by some sociologists

and an "organizational set" by others. See Chapter 2 for a discussion of the "role-set" concept from which the notion of organization set is drawn. The task environment includes all those elements in the organization's environment that have the potential to influence its performance or survival. One way to examine the task environment is to look for those places where the organization engages in some form of *exchange* with elements in the environment. Exchange can be defined as any voluntary or mandated act in which one party gives something in return for something else.

Agencies exchange clients, staff time, and expertise or services such as the conduct of surveys or the management of information. These exchanges need not be equal; it is only necessary that all parties to an exchange feel they benefit from it. When Agency A purchases the services of Agency B for some of A's clients, for example, the exchange may be totally unequal, yet of benefit to both. Agency A might also have the option to buy what it needs from a third agency, C. But Agency B may be totally dependent on A for its survival. But, the power relationship shifts if there is no C, and A has no alternative but to go to B.

Subtleties exist in this exchange process. Funders, for example, typically have a great deal of perceived power, but funders are also dependent on the agencies they fund. The United Fund may raise money for agencies that provide services. Through its allocating committees it may press a family agency to perform up to certain standards, but it may not be able to press too far. If those agencies it funds are not capable or willing to abide by United Fund guidelines, it will be in trouble. The United Fund, after all, is dependent on contributions from people who may like the family agency the way it is. The Fund has its own environment to worry about.

To understand the task environment, it is necessary to identify the key elements that affect your agency and its ability to perform all four functions described in Chapter 5. These elements need not interact with your agency directly. Their interactions with each other can result in an outcome that impacts on your agency.

The six elements of an agency's task environment are its (1) beneficiaries; (2) funders; (3) providers of nonfiscal resources; (4) providers of complementary services; (5) competitors; and (6) legitimators.

(1) *Beneficiaries* are those who receive services in direct and/or indirect ways. Clients in a hard drug treatment program who receive services are examples of direct beneficiaries. Families of ex-convicts who are using a job placement service are indirect beneficiaries of the service. They benefit from it, but only through the service provided the ex-prisoners.

(2) *Funders* provide money. Some funders provide an ongoing source of agency funds. These need not provide the largest amount of funding, however. A one-time grant may be larger than any allocation from a regular source.

(3) *Non-fiscal* resources vary from agency to agency. For example, free rent may be supplied by someone willing to donate space. In the second case, the agency is dependent upon volunteers to supply time and effort, and upon other agencies for referrals of those volunteers.

(4) *Providers of complementary services* are those individuals and organizations which provide other services to your agency's clients. A crisis center which refers to aged to protective services, to medical clinics, and to a mental health center, is using a number of complementary services. The detoxification unit in a hospital provides complementary services for an alcohol counseling center.

(5) *Competitors* are those programs outside your agency that need the same funds, legitimation, clients, or support from influentials in order to operate. They may provide the same service as your agency, or compete for funds from the same funding sources for different purposes.

(6) *Legitimation* comes from legislation, governmental bodies or your agency's board of directors. These may license an agency, give it accreditation, or an informal seal of approval. Sometimes, legitimation comes from individuals or organizations in the community. A judge, by referring offenders to an agency, implies its legitimacy. When professional associations endorse or certify agency staff, the legitimacy of that agency is increased in the public eye. Good public relations and a good press provide additional legitimation.

Interorganizational exchanges may take place between more than one organization at a given time. Exercises A and B are designed to help agency staff identify elements in its task environment and analyze the extent to which it is dependent on these elements. The exercises can be used to assess the power each element has over the agency. If, for example, an element of the task environment appears several times and in several categories, it is likely to be very important for your agency's survival or for the accomplishement of its goals. Task environment elements with high scores on the exercise are the organizations with whom your agency's relationships are most critical.

Read the instructions carefully. Then turn the page and carefully consider the illustration provided. Involve other staff, particularly those who peform "outward facing" tasks. Some knowledge of the environment or system of servies is necessary to complete the exercise. The more information you can bring to bear, the more complete the final picture will be.

EXERCISE A:
Managing the Organization's Environment

INSTRUCTIONS:

Examine the diagram of the elements in an agency's environment, its organization set. There is also a blank form for you to fill in.

1. Put your agency in the middle of the blank form.

2. List the organizations, groups, and individuals (units) with whom you or your agency interacts as the organization provides services or strives to maintain itself.

3. Place each organization, group or individual element under the appropriate major heading, for example, competitor, funder, and so on. It may appear in more than one place.

4. For each element (organization, group, individual), assess the amount of influence you think it has on the service delivery of your program or agency.

Assign a score to each unit from 5 points (equaling high influence) to 1 point (equaling low influence).

How many times and under which categories does an element appear on your picture? The more it appears, the more critical it may be.

Total the points accrued by each unit. Those with the highest scores will be the most critical elements in your environment.

Now, take this exercise, place your work unit in the middle, and do the same thing for the subunits within your agency.

Identify the organizational elements that have the greatest influence over your work unit within the total agency.

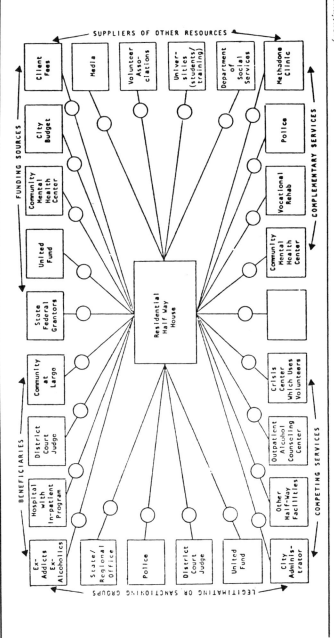

(continued)

85

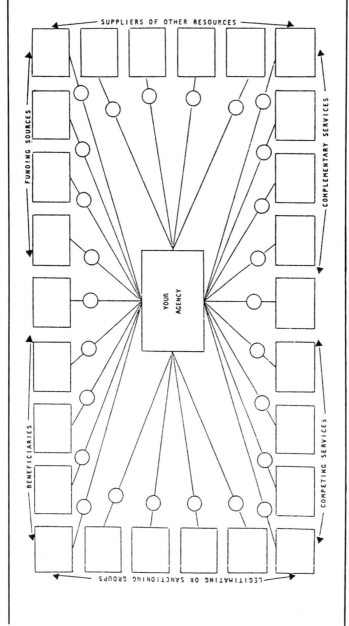

Figure 8   Sample of the Connections Between an Agency and Elements in its Task Environment

EXERCISE B:
Alternative Strategy Selection

INSTRUCTIONS:

Review the diagram you completed in Exercise A on a separate sheet of paper.

— List those units receiving *high* scores for frequency and importance.

— Think about which other groups could be *alternatives* to those on your list.

— Consider whether these alternatives might be reached in a short time frame and with minimal effort or disruption. Are there others that require a long-range developmental effort?

If immediate: What do you need to do to make the substitution? If long range; consider what you might do to effect the change, consider a potential time table; weigh the long-term gain against the short-term investment of resources.

Try out your ideas on other agency staff.

Now consider our earlier discussion on ecosystems. Identify at least three elements in the task environment in which the exchange relationship might be called symbiotic; three others in which the environment is clearly commensalistic. Are the relationships between your agency and others in its environment both commensalistic and symbiotic at the same time? How so? Describe.

WHERE DOES THIS PERSPECTIVE LEAD YOU?

If you focus on your agency's interaction with elements
in its task environment, you should be able to

— identify alternative sources of funds and legitimacy;

— be able to think through a variety of exchanges with potential
   providers of complementary services and providers of non-
   monetary resources;

— identify potential competitors for resources and legitimacy;

— anticipate changes in your agency's environment, and identify
   those changes that are crucial to your agency's survival and
   accomplishment of its service missions;

— identify those elements in the environment that need your
   services as you need theirs (symbiosis) and those which have
   similar or identical missions and methods that might be better
   met through cooperation with your agency (commensalism);

— specify those internal and external factors that, when mediated
   by new technology, are likely to create significant pressures
   (and opportunities) for change.

STRENGTHS AND LIMITS
OF USING THIS PERSPECTIVE

Strengths	Limits
It defines an entire network of services.	Relationships may be seen as competitive, when in fact they may only be uncoordinated.
It allows an agency to analyze its position with regard to other agencies, groups, and individuals.	
It may lead to identifying potentially rewarding interorganizational exhanges.	It focuses on organizational interaction rather than service delivery to clients.
It makes possible (and may even promote) the coordination of services to clients.	
It can help an agency identify where community resources are located and who needs or competes for these resources.	
It can define potential trouble spots with outside agencies and allow for planning for the change in impact this will have on your agency.	

Chapter 7

YOUR AGENCY AS A PEOPLE-CHANGING AND PEOPLE-PROCESSING SYSTEM

In Chapter 5 we spoke of resources as "inputs" and services as "products" or "outputs." We referred to the functions of each of the agency's subsystems in relation to these inputs and outputs. For example, we described the production subsystem's function as taking such resources as money and personnel and transforming these into services. In this chapter we will explore a rather different perspective. Resources will be expanded to include the agency's "raw materials," those persons who are to be processed or changed. The output will be defined as their changed status and position or their changed behavior. Put more accurately the agency's output is "people with changed statuses or behaviors."[1] Thus, those people we have been accustomed to thinking of as recipients or consumers (clients, students, members, patients) will now be defined as raw materials to be shaped or otherwise acted upon. Lest the term "raw materials" seem a bit crass, let me point out that by shifting to this orientation, we also shift our definition of product from services to outcomes, from means to ends. In so doing we elevate rather than denigrate the individuals who pass through our agencies.

STAFF-CLIENT RELATIONSHIPS

For simplicity's sake we'll refer to all those people who are processed or shaped by a social agency as *clients.* These include students, welfare recipients, hospital patients, community centers members, prison inmates, persons subject in one way or another to court rulings, and the like. We'll refer to those persons assigned to working with them (providing some form of agency service) as *staff.* Staff-client relationships are at the core of all activities in social agencies; they are central to the agency's missions; they are its definition of what it is in business for.

These relationships are aimed, from the staff's point of view, at either categorizing the client and his or her needs, or at changing the client in some way. The more critical the need or the more significant the change sought, the more important the nature of the relationship and the demands made of the client. From the client's point of view the agency and his or her relationship to a member of its staff is aimed at securing some sought after benefit: a change in status or position; greater access to needed resources; more control over his or her circumstances; perhaps even the instrinsic value inherent in the relationship, one that increases the client's sense of belonging, self-esteem, or pleasure in social intercourse. If the client perceives the nature of the relationship to be less than beneficial, even punitive, he or she may attempt to manipulate it somewhat, controlling the degree of information provided, refusing to cooperate or circumventing agency rules, perhaps opting out of the relationship altogether.

Clients are, after all, people, each with his or her own identity, only a part of which is connected in some way to the agency. Clients have their own values, characteristic patterns of behavior, goals, and objectives. If they are not forced to accept agency services (for example, by court order or out of desperation), they can always resist the agency's efforts to categorize them or to change them.

The agency is always limited in its ability to coerce or demand compliance. For example, a university may set up rules and procedures for satisfactory completion of academic requirements, but short of refusing to award a degree, it can do little to force students to comply. A physician on a hospital staff can recommend surgery, but short of emergency procedures, cannot force the patient to accept the recommendation. The more important the agency's service is to the client and the less likely he or she can find a substitute elsewhere, the more likely that the client will comply. The greater the need for the client's willing compliance, the more likely the agency will accommodate to the client's perception of appropriate demands and services. This is especially true if clients represent or are affiliated with prestigious or influential social groups.

These limitations on the agency's authority require that it establish procedures to minimize conflict in staff-client relationships and increase staff control over those relationships. This they can do by appealing to common values ("We both want you to get well," "Education is important," "If we work together we can make this center the kind of place we want it to be"), by pointing out the benefits of compliance ("If you register, we can assure you that the checks will keep coming on a monthly basis"), or by threatening dire consequences for noncompliance ("If you don't attend group sessions, I'll have to report you to the probation department...sorry, but those are the rules")[2] Staff can also control the relationship through the establishment and maintenance of a set of procedures that keep the client at a certain distance and with limited access to information ("We'll meet here every Wednesday at 3." "Sorry, that's priviledged information," or "When you've been here a while, you'll get to understand").

PEOPLE PROCESSING

People processing organizations (or processing units within a more comprehensive service organization) are in the business of turning people into clients (such as students, members, recipients, patients, graduates, and so on). Their principle functions are to classify people and to confer on them new statuses. For example, a welfare office or social security office might classify potential clients as having the rights to certain services or benefits. A university admissions office might classify a student for regular or conditional admissions or for advance standing. A community referral center might diagnose a client's problems and refer the client to the appropriate agency or practitioner for service. A placement office might certify a trainee's completion of training and refer him or her to one or more jobs. In each of these examples the processing results in a particular classification or status that others (who might then provide benefits or services) would understand.

Of necessity, such processing can deal with only some aspects of the total person. And in practice it is done through a number of stages common to most social agencies. These include (1) assessment of the client's attributes and circumstances to decide whether he or she can legitimately be served by the agency or by others on whose behalf the agency is working; (2) exploring both those attributes and circumstances to determine appropriate action alternatives; (3) choosing between those alternatives; and (4) referring or placing the client in a location where his or her classification or altered status will result in requisite services or benefits. These stages can be further reduced to a set of steps: (1) reception; (2) recording; (3) labeling; (4) routing; (5) treating; and (6) referral or discharge.

In this process the client often feels as if he or she has been turned into "nothing but a piece of paper." Becoming a client is, in fact, becoming an artifact of the agency. Regardless of rhetoric or ideology, the agency is *never* interested in the whole person. The agency *is* interested in those characteristics of the person that make it possible to serve or refer the person (change the person or process the person); in other words, to transform the person into a client. And this invariably requires paper (or a computerized substitute).

Paper is used to record client characteristics, progress, diagnosis (labels), recommendations, and so on. Staff access to these papers and their ability to withold or to make them available to scrutiny or to use them to issue reports gives staff considerable control over clients. For their parts, clients are likely to reveal only what they perceive will yield them a net benefit. They often attempt to present those characteristics that are most likely to result in favorable treatment. Think of how you have filled out college application forms, job applications, or applications for membership in an organization, and you will know what I mean. If you are on the staff side, you know how bothersome it can be when forms are relatively ambiguous or when they include information that you don't need (information that may be very significant to the client, but not relevant in terms of the services that your agency is ready or able to dispense). In fact, asking for irrelevant information is often perceived as an unjustified intrusion into the individual's privacy. Thus both worker and client may conspire (agree) to a procedure that reduces the client to the characteristics recorded on paper.

EXERCISE A

People Processing

Identify the steps or procedures that are linked together in the processing of a client in an agency with which you are familiar. Spell out what happens in each step:

—reception (who, by whom, when, where)

—recording (what, for what purpose)

—labeling (describe categories)

—routing (by whom, to whom)

—treating or educating (describe briefly)

—referral or discharge (when, how)

Feel free to modify the steps to reflect the situation in the agency you are describing.

PEOPLE CHANGING

In addition to these processing functions, many social agencies also engage in a program of people changing through education and socialization or through some form of treatment. As noted, the end product of the agency's service is a changed (generally improved) person. That improvement may include being better educated or competant to practice a profession, cured of a disease, rehabilitated, financially self-sufficient, able to live independently, and so on. Thus the service provided is defined as part of the agency's throughput system rather than as its output. The client who is to undergo change is perceived as raw material to be molded, refined, or otherwise improved and supported in some way.

Vinter (1963) distinguishes socialization oriented organizations such as schools, youth agencies, senior centers, settlement houses from treatment agencies such as mental hospitals, child guidance clinics, training programs for the chronically unemployed, drug maintenance programs along three dimensions. These are the clients they serve, the nature of the changes sought, and the assessment of each accorded by the larger society.

Socialization and education organizations such as schools and universities generally receive considerable legitimation in part because of the populations they serve, and in part because it is assumed that their clients are willingly involved in the process of change towards some socially acceptable goal—getting a degree or getting a job. Persons served in some treatment oriented agencies, such as general hospitals, are also presumed to want to get better, but in any case are not to be blamed for their problems or defects. They are, after all, only victims of ill health. And any of us could, and probably will, spend time in a hospital.

The same is not necessarily true of those in mental hospitals and in other agencies perceived as being in the business of changing people because of some moral defect—their deviation from the norms of behavior society imposes on them. In addition to the mentally ill, delinquents, criminals, the poor, and the chronically unemployed are regarded by society as being improperly motivated or possessing otherwise defective attributes. Those organizations charged with changing them are regarded by the general public with some of the same disapproval as their clientele, Yet paradoxically these agencies are given much greater latitude in the methods, and in particular the coercive methods they can use to promote compliance with behavioral norms. Thus the agencies with the toughest jobs may get the least public approval for doing their work unless they, too, "get tough."

MOVING FROM RAW MATERIALS
TO THE FINAL PRODUCT

There are some real conceptual and programmatic advantages to looking at an agency's clientele as its raw material to be processed or changed in some way. Focusing on the outcome (of either processing or socialization and treatment) rather than on the services an agency provides makes it possible to address the purposes for which the agency was established.

Nevertheless, the implied parallel between a factory or production unit that utilizes raw materials and social agencies does not hold 100 percent. First of all, the agency's raw material, as we have seen, interacts with agency staff and others to determine the final outcome. That outcome is never solely the result of the agency's efforts, even when there is full compliance on the part of the client. The process of change (whether in desired or undesired directions), continues throughout the former client's lifetime, often long after processing or treatment has ceased.

Second, the agency's technology, the methods it uses, is likely to be much less precise, repeatable, and effective than those employed in a manufacturing plant. We generally know what to expect when we apply heat or force to an inanimate material. We have very little knowledge of cause and effect relations when it comes to human behavior. In fact, the complexity of the tasks faced by most agencies causes them to limit what they do and how. That very limitation, while increasing some degree of efficiency, is likely to result in some loss of effectiveness. Because these limited means may be applicable only to certain clients, they may require a screening process in which those most likely to succeed are screened in and others screened out. This is what vocational rehabilitation agencies often referred to as "creaming" or "skimming the cream off the top."

A third problem lies in the ambiguity of most agency goals and in particular the treatment goals they set for their clients. Because goals are statements of intent, they specify values. Often these are values around which there is no universal agreement. In fact, there are likely to be multiple and conflicting expectations of the agency by various elements in what we have earlier described as the task environment (see Chapter 6). The lack of consensus on goals is also found within the agency; different professional groups and different departments may hold views that are at variance with each other. Finally, as we have seen, both clients and staff are apt to seek different outcomes from their relationship. Their perceptions of appropriate outcomes may change over the course of that relationship.

These problems make it exceedingly difficult to develop useful outcome measures. If goals are ambiguous and technology is indeterminate, it becomes almost impossible to define the criteria for measurement of effectiveness. And if there are variables that can effect the client's behavior during and subsequent to the agency-directed change process, then it becomes virtually impossible to measure, with total validity, the impact of the agency's efforts to change the client.

EXERCISE B

People Changing (Treatment or Education)

1. Who changes whom in an agency you are familiar with? List all the possibilities.
2. To what extent is this change effort empirically based? ideologically based? Explain.
3. How does the agency try to control client-worker interactions (rules, procedures, schedules, location, etc.)? Explain.
4. How do clients influence the process? How central are they to its outcome? What can they do to facilitate or subvert it?

WHERE DOES THIS PERSPECTIVE LEAD YOU?

If you hold that the agency is involved in people changing and people processing and that its clients are the raw materials of this process, then you might

— redirect your focus from agency activities to the outcomes of those activities;

— examine what the client brings in terms of aspirations and capacities to the staff-client relationship;

— tailor paper work and recording to the client's needs and less to those of the agency and the other consumer of its services (those to whom it refers clients, those who provide other needed resources);

— differentiate between socialization ;and treatment in the design of agency programs, and involve the client more fully in both processes;

— work on increasing public support for both the clientele and the methods used with agency clients, particularly if the public's perceptions are counter-productive because of misperceptions and biases.

STRENGTHS AND LIMITS
OF USING THIS PERSPECTIVE

Strengths	Limits
Viewing clients as "raw materials" puts the focus on where it ought to be: on the people whose personal aspirations, vested interests, capacities, and needs are the raison d'être of the agency's operations.	The term "raw material," if used without heed to the fact that clients are human beings, may lead to viewing them as neutral and inanimate objects whose resistance is to be overcome rather than perceived as a legitimate part of the goal setting and growth processes.
A focus on people processing brings with it the recognition that diagnosis and categorization should lead to seeking alternative socialization and treatment modalities.	A premature or overly rigid labeling process may preclude examination of the range of alternative goals and means that should be used.
Understanding that processing leads to referral increases the likelihood that agency personnel will engage in negotiations with elements in the environment to whom clients may be sent, leading to a more appropriate or comprehensive service program.	Over-concern with "marketing the product" may result in serving the needs of those who subsequently work with the client, rather than the client himself or herself.
Recognizing that people changing activities include both socialization and education, a more appropriate mix of the two may be developed.	

Strengths	Limits
This perspective also makes it likely that agency staff will focus on outcomes in terms of client statuses and behaviors, rather than on the process by which these take place.	Concern with outcomes may obscure the fact that both the technology used and the goals sought may be indeterminate and ambiguous.

NOTES

1. I am indebted for many of these concepts to my colleague, Yeheskel Hasenfeld, of the University of Michigan.

2. Amitai Etzioni (1961), a sociologist from Columbia University, has referred to these as *normative, utilitarian,* and *coercive* compliance systems.

3. For a detailed analysis of these steps, and for further discussion of turning people into paper, see Prottas (1980).

Chapter 8

YOUR AGENCY AS THE CONTEXT WITHIN WHICH TECHNOLOGIES ARE APPLIED

The work "technology" refers to a complex of activities performed by individuals on some object to be changed or processed. It generally requires a well-developed knowledge base that anticipates the consequences of one action or another. It may or may not require mechanical devices, but it always requires some form of tool. For example, in computer technology we employ software (or the program, which is essentially a complex of ideas and instructions) and hardware (the physical computer itself and related devices).

Organizations provide the context within which technologies are applied to a variety of objects. In fact they employ many technologies in order to do their business more efficiently and with a certain degree of rationality, the presumption being that by doing X, we get Y. These technologies are related to each of the functions of an organization we explored in Chapter 5: production, adaptation, boundary maintenance, and management. In both the management and adaptive subsystems, for example, we employ a variety of budgeting and accounting technologies, social indicators, operations research, and other information gathering and processing technologies (often organized into management information systems referred to as MIS), and personnel management technologies (including task analysis and job design, staff development, and training). In boundary maintenance we may use public relations, fund raising, and contracting of a variety of interagency linkages.

But the central or core technologies, those with which our agencies are identified and which provide them with their "social" or "human service" identities, are those associated with the production subsystem. And it is these, interestingly enough, that provide us with the greatest difficulties. The precision aimed for in other technologies is hard to come by in our efforts to serve people. Although clients may be defined as an agency's raw materials, they are not without wills of their own. Many human service technologies, in fact, require that agency clientele be regarded as subjects and full participants in the service program, rather than as objects to be worked on.

TECHNOLOGY IN THE HUMAN SERVICES

James D. Thompson (1967) a seminal thinker among organizational theorists, described organizational technologies as being *long-linked* (such as on the assembly line), *mediating* (as in negotiations or information dissemination), and *intensive* (as in teaching or treatment). These concepts will serve us well in our examination of your agency as the context within which technologies are applied.

The reason that teaching and treatment are defined as intensive is that a variety of techniques may be used independently or in concert to effect change in the object; in this case, individual or collectivities of human beings. Moreover, these "objects" of the actions taken are, in fact, "subjects," persons who, through their reactions, responses and initiatives, provide feedback to those applying the technology, often shaping the way in which it is applied.

The intensiveness of human service work is directly related to two variables. One is the nature of the work being done. For example, treatment or "people changing" tends in general to be more intensive than intake or referral (which we referred to in Chapter 7 as "people processing"). The individual being treated is likely to be acted upon in more ways than the person being processed. When that person, in turn, acts on the process, he or she becomes an integral partner to it. The second variable is related to the prevalence of "exceptional" cases; that is, the extent to which each client or client system presents problems to be worked on that are unique and that require a specially tailored complex of intervention activities.

If the nature of the agency's work with clients is such that a great deal of reaction is expected of the client (as in rehabilitation counseling, family treatment, child guidance, and some forms of job training), then considerable discretion may be given the worker with regards to how to respond and to shape the client's behavior. The same is true if the client's reactions are likely to be unpredictable (as in psychotherapy). The worker, or the department, may be given considerable latitude in the design of interventions and in the techniques used. Idiosyncratic and unpredictable behavior, after all, requires nonroutine responses. But the lack of routine response runs counter to the logic of organization, and for this reason most social agencies attempt to develop routine ways of responding to nonroutine events.

They do so in two ways. First, social agencies create routines that are based on specific tasks, to be performed by specially designated staff in set ways; and, second, they create ideological frameworks that guide the social worker in his or her interactions with clients.

DEVELOPING ROUTINE RESPONSES

Social agencies, like all formal organizations, find it hard to live with uncertainty. Thus they establish sets of rules and procedures that determine who they will serve (what kinds of clients with what kinds of problems), who will provide the service (needed training or other qualifications), the kinds of service or other activities they will perform, and at what level of intensity. They engage in a deliberate structuring of the client-staff relationship. Sometimes this is accomplished by "departmentalizing" services and related activities. Various aspects are broken down into component parts; each of these is assigned to different work units or departments. A hospital is a good example of an organization that provides intensive care through various substructures: radiology, pathology, surgery, social work, and so on.

This is characteristic of many agencies that engage in people changing activities. Other organizations serialize service, much as is done on an assembly line. A client first goes through intake, then through assessment, then is routed for service (sometimes in a number of different units for different problems or needs), and finally is referred elsewhere or is discharged. This is most characteristic of people processing organizations.

The greater the breakdown of tasks and their assignment to specialized units, the more the need for coordination and related administrative supports. Because service tasks are generally concrete and specific, the worker's judgments are limited to specific issues, and the staff-client relationship is set within bounds. Moreover, formalized relationships are also established between staff and between departments as ways of supporting the controls and limitations on staff-client interactions. You will find that such organizations tend to go by the rules or follow the book on procedures. They tend to have formal communication patterns and tall structures with numerous layers of supervision so as to assure compliance with the rules. This is especially necessary when the staff are narrowly trained, each prepared to perform only limited tasks. In such organizations both rules and structure are designed so as to assure a modicum of uniformity in activity or outcome.

In contrast, there are other types of social agencies (such as women's crisis centers or psychiatric clinics) in which uncertainty cannot easily be controlled for. The same may be true of subunits within a more formal organization. This uncertainty is often present when client responsiveness is integral to the treatment technology. In such circumstances a good deal of discretion may be given to each staff person who is expected to perform many tasks with or on behalf of the client. Because much less coordination is needed when multiple responsibilities are vested in a single worker, such agencies or subunits are characterized by a much flatter structure and less bureaucracy, by which is meant less administration and fewer layers between top management and worker. These organizations are further characterized by a colleagal management style. Workers tend to be more highly trained in expectation that such training will enable them to make independent judgments professionally, (i.e., based on knowledge and guided by an ethical code).

IDEOLOGICAL FRAMEWORKS

But rules are easily subverted, and a profession's knowledge base may not be adequately grounded empirically. Some other means of assuring compliance with what the agency considers to be good practice may be required. This can be achieved through commitment to an ideology, a belief system about what is morally correct and what works. Such norms might be developed outside the agency (as in a professional school) and borrowed with some adaptation. They can also be the result either of a conscious decision within the agency or the result of joint experience over a period of years. Often such norms or belief systems are imbedded in the practice methodology employed. Thus, in social work, a number of norms are build into the training of caseworkers, group practitioners, community organizers, and others. These include commitments to client self-determination, confidentiality, participation in treatment and change, and so on. And these commitments are expressed in the treatment modalities employed.

Although the agency can to a certain degree assure compliance with desired norms through the employment of staff who are trained in the appropriate professions, there may be times when professional norms and agency norms are in conflict. In such cases, if the agency does not institute bureaucratic rules and procedures to assure compliance with desired norms of behavior, it may attempt to develop service ideologies of its own. This becomes especially important if the service technology cannot guarantee desired results; that is, if the knowledge base upon which it is founded does not show direct relationships between the means used and the outcomes desired (cause and effect). This is certainly true in most psychotherapies and in many other areas where intensive treatment of the client is required. Such ideologies are composed of beliefs about the client, the causes of the problem that brought the problem to the agency, and the consequences of prescribed actions.

Because beliefs are often based on value commitments rather than empirical evidence, they tend to provide the rationale for methods that cannot be justified technically. And for this reason, too, they tend to be emotionally binding. Because they give coherence to the agency's methodologies, any challenge of the belief system tends also to be seen as a challenge to the agency itself. Accepting these beliefs is demonstration of identification with the agency. A commitment to the agency is interpreted as a commitment to its ideal of service. The stronger the belief system, the more self-confirming and difficult to challenge. Neverless in the absence of more empirically grounded technologies, and in response to the sometimes overly bureaucratized and fragmented (some say "dehumanized") approaches of other agencies, those with strong ideological commitments may be well received by both clients and the general public.

EXERCISE A
Intensive and Long-Linked Technologies

1. Examine an intensive treatment technology in your agency or in another agency you may be familiar with. Now break it down into serial steps so that is is organized in a long-linked manner. Refer to Exercises A and B in Chapter 7, if you wish.

   What are the advantages and disadvantages to the agency of such restructuring? to the worker? to the client?

2. Now take a long-linked technology and redesign it as an intensive process.

   What are the advantages and disadvantages to the agency? to the worker? to the client?

3. What are the implications of such changes for:

   — the agency's formal structure;
   — staff training or professional background;
   — the agency's relationships to key publics (clients, funders, auspice providers, cooperating or competing agencies)?

THE PROBLEM OF
INCOMPATIBLE TECHNOLOGIES

No agency is limited to a single, inclusive technology. In most situations a great number of technologies operate side by side; sometimes they operate in near total concert, more often with considerable strain in their relationships. This strain may be due to (1) ideological incompatibility; (2) an inappropriate effort to import and transform to the human services technologies developed for other purposes; (3) the challenges imposed by the rigor of technologies not belonging to the human services also used in the agency; (4) the fact that knowledge available through everyday means may prove more useful for some interventions than knowledge gained from some form of professional or occupational training (we'll call this the "challenge of nontechnologies"); and (5) incompatibility with the clients themselves.

Ideological incompatibility seems to be greater in those situations where competing technologies are the most indeterminant; that is, when they deal with difficult social psychological problems for which no clear criteria for the measurement of success exist. In fact, the closer they are to each other in substance, the more difficult it may be for practitioners to arrive at some accommodation with each other. That is why some of the proponents of various neo-Freudian schools of psychotherapy are in such violent disagreement with each other (as were Freud's disciples).

Technological incompatibility may be even more visible, at least after the fact, when methods borrowed from other fields are applied to the human services without an understanding of the basic differences in their foundations. For example, in the late 1960s and well into the 1970s there were serious efforts to shape, bend, and even impose program planning and budgeting systems (PPBS) on the operations of social agencies. PPBS was developed in the Department of Defense, and based on an industry model. It had its difficulties even there because it requires prior consensus on goals and operational objectives. These are perhaps the most difficult to define in the human services. As we will see in the next chapter, it may not even be appropriate to seek total clarity, much less consensus. Even those technologies borrowed from one human service endeavor and applied to another may not fit. Thus, efforts to apply behavior treatment technologies to agency management and to community work may be totally misguided, because so little in the environment is subject to the control of those attempting the intervention.

The challenges imposed by technologies not developed for human services used in human service agencies may be even more difficult to accommodate. For example, the new information processing technologies, computer based as they are, required reporting of inputs, throughputs, and outcomes in such a way as to seriously challenge human service ideologies and to force them to report only that which is clearly measurable. New accounting and budgeting procedures require shifting focus from what money is spend *on* (as in line-item budgeting) to what it is spent *for* (as in performance budgeting, which often focuses on the cost of achieving a given objective). Program evaluation and other operations research efforts may likewise focus on outcomes, often obfuscating or ignoring immeasurables the program staff believe are central to their efforts. Such challenges are not necessarily bad. To the contrary, uncomfortable as they may be, they are frequently the stimulus needed to eliminate wasteful effort and to sharpen the focus of social intervention. But they are difficult to accommodate.

By the challenge of nontechnologies I mean those common sense, everyday methods that may be much more appropriate than high-cost therapies or other methods that require intensive professional training. Thus the loneliness of the aged might better be treated by a volunteer home visit network than through pyschotherapy in a physician's or social worker's office.

Finally, we come to the issue of the interdependence of human service technologies and the attributes of the client. Many of the methods of intervention developed by human service professions are based on insight, psychological understanding, the ability to communicate—a repertoire of skills that have a clear middle-class bias, especially when used by middle-class practitioners who may be tuned into the psyches of their clients, but not to their class ethnic, social, or cultural lifestyles and the repertoire of skills that accompany those patterns of behavior and response. This bias leads to blaming the client, defining him or her as unresponsive, hostile, or unmotivated.

EXERCISE B
Technological Incompatibility

1. Describe briefly one or more agency technologies that are incompatible with (a) strongly held beliefs of the staff (ideologies); (b) human service objectives borrowed uncritically from some other field; (c) clients and their needs, interests, or capacities.
2. Could these technologies be made more compatible? How? If not, what alternatives exist?

WHERE DOES THIS PERSPECTIVE LEAD YOU?

When you view the agency as the context within which a number of technologies are applied, you might

— focus on those technologies that are core to the agency's purposes, that give the agency its identity as a human service organization; and distinguish these from others that are intended to facilitate (rather than shape or redefine) the human service function;

— distinguish between those technologies that are long-linked, mediating, or intensive, and design the agency structure to accommodate these differences, rather than the other way around (adapting technology to fit the agency structure);

— recognize the unique contribution that the client as subject can make to the processing or treatment activities the agency engages in, so that the client is not perceive of and acted upon solely as an object (with all the dehumanization implied);

— sharpen up the knowledge base of the core technologies used (in particular cause and effect relationships); but when this is not possible because of the inherent indeterminacy of the technology, recognize the limitations of both the rules and the ideologies used to impose control and standardization on those technologies, perhaps through setting up an evaluation and review process that looks not only at individual cases, but that challenges the basic assumptions that underly those technologies.

STRENGTHS AND LIMITS
OF USING THIS PERSPECTIVE

Strengths	Limits
It permits focus on the core activities for which the agency was established and its programs created.	It can be diverting, focusing on nonproduction related technologies, because these are more controllable and seem to yield more precise and predictable outcomes.
It recognizes the indeterminacy of many human services technologies and so reduces the likelihood of inappropriate expectations.	By focusing on the technology itself, it may obscure the client as subject, focusing inappropriately on the client as object, without will and personality.
By identifying those technologies that require long-linked, mediating, or intensive actions, it makes it possible to divide or consolidate tasks appropriately and to design the agency structure accordingly.	
By recognizing that ideology is not only a way of assuring quality for responsible behavior on the part of the practitioner, but also tends to be self-confirming, it increases the likelihood that emotionally binding beliefs about practice will be subject to review and reassessment.	In an effort to "objectify" practice and to reduce the importance of ideology the agency may establish a set of procedures intended to assure quality services and efficiency, but in fact further reducing the client to an object.

Chapter 9

YOUR AGENCY AS A
GOAL-SEEKING ORGANIZATION

Organizations are goal seeking enterprises, designed and built to achieve specified ends. It follows that if there is consensus on goals and if these goals are realistic and precise, it should be possible to properly engineer an organization to achieve its goals. Unfortunately, in most social agencies goals are not necessarily realistic or precise, nor is there universal consensus about their appropriateness. These difficulties are in the nature of both social agencies and goals. The reasons for such difficulties will become clear as we examine the nature of goals, their functions, and the ways in which they are developed.

GOALS AND THE FUNCTIONS THEY PERFORM

According to Etzioni (1964), goals provide (1) the directions or aims that organizations must have in order to be purposive; (2) the standards against which the agency and its activities are evaluated; and (3) legitimacy for both directions and activities. Organizations have stated goals, those that indicate officially what they intend to accomplish. They also have unofficial, sometimes hidden, but "real" goals; those toward which most of their significant resources and energies are directed.

When referring to the total organization, in contrast with more specific operations, goals are framed in the most general terms and always reflect the organization's sense of mission—that which legitimates its efforts. These may include advancement of knowledge (a university); strengthening family life (a family service agency); or providing dignity for the aged (a community center). At this level of generality, goals are "safe" and relatively uncontroversial. They can energize, as any symbol might, but they are not sufficiently precise to provide operational guidelines or to serve as standards against which achievements can be evaluated. Efforts to make overall goals more precise would lead to disagreements among an agency's staff and supporters and limit the agency's ability to shift gears. Nevertheless, the elaboration of ends and means is essential when we move from the general to the more operational levels of the organization. I'll explain.

ENDS AND MEANS ELABORATION:
A RATIONAL APPROACH

Suppose you wanted to establish your own agency, or a program within an existing organization. If you were using rational and purposive design approach, you might employ a procedure to

(1) examine all aspects of the situation in which you find yourself—the needs or problems to be addressed, the available resources, the extent to which there is support for action;

(2) select a general goal or goals to aim for;

(3) list all the possible means for achieving each goal; check to see if the necessary resources are available or if the costs are too high for each; examine the consequences of pursuing one course of action or another; and

(4) select the means that are the most feasible, acceptable, or desirable.

The means selected then become subgoals, and their identification leads to further listing of means. The process continues from the most general of goals to those that are the most specific. This has sometimes been called the "branching tree" or "root" method of planning (Lindblom, 1959). At the end of the process we get to the most operational goals, those that provide specific guides to action and are measurable in terms of outcome. At these levels the operative goals are generally called "operational objectives." In turn, these can be phrased in terms of operations, activities, and outcomes.

For example, suppose one of the subgoals of a family service agency (whose generally goal is the "enhancement of family life," a goal that is hardly subject to controversy or to evaluation), is to "reduce family violence" (both a means toward the more general objective and a subgoal in its own right). Here are what some operational objectives might look like:

— *operations objective*—Thirty volunteers will be recruited, trained, and assigned to monitor and answer telephone and walk-in requests for help of an emergency nature, in sufficient hours to cover all requests.

— *activity objective*—By the end of the first year, four self-help groups will have been organized to operate with minimal assistance from the agency, and between four and six others will be in various stages of development.

— *outcome objective*—The rate of reported incidents of family violence in the south/central district will be reduced by 25% within a twelve-month period.

Clearly, each of these is a means toward achieving more general goals, but each is also a subgoal. The following exercise will give you a better idea of how the branching tree process works. It begins with a general problem and progresses to the specification of intervention approaches. In the example given, the general problem and the goals identified presume some more overarching and even more general goals that sanction and define the purposes of the agency. At the lower level of the tree, the intervention alternatives and even the program components might also be phrased as subgoals. Schematically, the process is presented in the following figure.

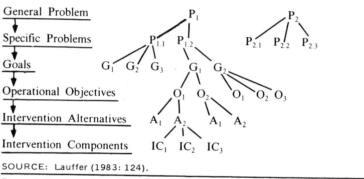

General Problem

Specific Problems

Goals

Operational Objectives

Intervention Alternatives

Intervention Components

SOURCE: Lauffer (1983: 124).

Figure 9 The Branching Tree Process

Now try the exercise.

EXERCISE
The Branching Tree

(1) Start with one or more general problems. For example:

P_j | Many of the elderly in Corktown have difficulty with personal management. This is especially severe with the single aged.

(2) Then break it down into its component parts; make the problem more specific in relation to targeted groups of the elderly. These specific problems might include:

$P_{1.1}$ | Nutritional Deficiencies

$P_{1.2}$ | Poor management of personal budgets.

$P_{1.3}$ | Inability to do basic housekeeping or to perform household repairs.

$P_{1.4}$ | Difficulty in getting about for purposes of shopping or getting to service providers.

(3) Use these more specific problems to establish your goals. For example, "nutritional deficiencies" might result in your determining that:

G_1 | Older people, particularly those isolated in rural areas, will be fed nutritiously.

(4) Now it is time to define your operational objectives.* The following might be included:

O_1 | Eighty percent of the persons in the target area will receive information about diets and how they can manage nutritious eating programs on a limited budget.

O_2 | Prepared foods, at an affordable cost will be available close to home to 500 people by the end of the second year of the project's operation.

(5) How might these objectives be reach? Let us take the second objective. Service alternatives might include:

A_1 | Meals-on-Wheels Home Delivery.

A_2 | Congregate meal sites at local schools and churches.

A_3 | Cooperative cooking programs in conjunction with the Coop Food Buying program.

(6) Each of these requires a number of service components. The meals-on-wheels alternative, for example, might require:

IC_1 | Outreach and case finding of potential elderly participants.

IC_2 | Sites at which food can be prepared.

IC_3 | A nutritionist who can design menus and supervise meal preparation.

IC_4 | Volunteers for food preparation and transportation to homes.

SOURCE: Adapted from an approach developed by Yeheskel Hasenfeld and originally published in Lauffer (1983: 124-125).
*Review earlier discussion of operations, activity, and outcome objectives.

Goal setting, when described in this way, is both purposive and rational. Unfortunately, while goal setting is always a more or less purposive process, it is rarely all that rational. First of all, we can never be certain we have considered all the possible means. Second, even for those considered, we seldom have sufficient information to assess properly the consequence of selecting one means or another. As you will recall from our early discussion of organizational technologies (Chapter 8), the understanding of cause and effect relationships in the human services (and social sciences in general) is skimpy at best.

Even more important, means have a way of shaping goals, perhaps more than the other way around. John Dewey used to say that we set up targets to "facilitate the act of shooting" rather than "shoot to hit the target." Thus we expand hospital facilities to be able to install more advanced technology, or we declare high sounding research and service missions for our universities to provide the organizational supports for and structure through which faculty and others can perform the work they have trained for.

Some administrators and program planners argue that rather than proceding from the most general to the most specific along the branching tree, the procedure should be reversed. Once the agency has decided what it is going to do or taken stock of what it is doing, it must justify those activities. A particular affirmative action program may generate controversy, but most citizens would agree to the legitimacy of "increasing access to opportunity." Open classrooms might be controversial, but "improving the quality of education" is not. To the contrary, these more general goals are such that all of us can rally to them. They promise much and so serve not only to define the overall purposes of our agencies, but to legitimate their activities, and to provide the energizing concept around which support for those activities can be emergized.

The vagueness of these goals are both their advantage and disadvantage. Because high sounding goals can never be fully achieved, they rarely have to be changed, so they provide stability over time. An oft-quoted exception to this rule is found in the example of the March of Dimes. After polio was nearly wiped out, the organization no longer had a function. A new set of goals had to be found in order to give the agency a purpose around which its superb machinery could be focused. It now raises money for the study of birth defects and related development disabilities. The disadvantage of vagueness, however, is that it makes it virtually impossible to measure results. The further one moves along the branching tree to concreteness of means and objectives, the more goals are subject to measurement and evaluation.

MEASURING GOAL ATTAINMENT

Two measures are generally used: effectiveness and efficiency. Effectiveness refers to how close end results are to stated goals and objectives. Efficiency refers to what it costs in resources (time, personnel, money) to achieve the goal. Here, one should be careful. First, for each objective pursued, others may have been neglected or set aside, and these others may have been more relevant to the overall stated on official goal of the agency. Second, in the human services as in other "industries," one should recognize that efficiency is a relative term.

Etzioni (1964) points out that a light bulb converts only 5 percent of the electrical energy it consumes into light. The rest is dissipated as heat. Should we then disgard light bulbs because they are inefficient; or should we compare one manufacturer's light bulbs against another's, perhaps valuing one that converts 5.5 percent of its energy into light in contrast with a less efficient product that manages only 4.5 percent efficiency? Should social agencies be evaluated on more stringent criteria? Are they to be judged inefficient if they do not achieve 90 or 100 percent of the objective sought? Or should we not establish goal achievement scales on which we can make judgments on a comparative basis?

I want to point out a danger in measuring goal attainment. If attainments are measurable, we are likely to measure them. We are less likely to attempt to measure those that are not easily subjected to evaluation. Thus, measurement focuses attention on some goals and not on others. And those that are the center of attention are often valued above others. The clearer the goals are, the greater the propensity to engage in activities directed at those goals, because rewards and penalties for achievement can be attached to them. For this reason, highly programmed tasks, those governed by hard and fast rules, tend to drive out more ambiguous ones that are harder to justify (unless as you will recall from the chapter on technology, they are envigorated by a strong belief system). This may result in spending more time and energy on activities that are less directly related to the more general goals or purposes of the organization, or focusing on some goals to the exclusion of others.

GOAL DISTORTION, DISPLACEMENT, AND SUCCESSION

For example, focusing on the improvement of math or reading scores in the fifth grade may result in neglect of character development and group problem solving. Measuring job training programs on the basis of numbers of formerly unemployed persons placed on jobs may result in drawing the cream off the top or in a neglect of the trainee's other needs (e.g., job satisfaction, career opportunity, status, and pay). Likewise, an emphasis on placing "hard-to-place" children in adoptive homes may ignore the suitability of those homes for children with special needs.

Insidious as this process of goal distortion may be, it is more easily corrected than goal displacement. For example, when agency management becomes more concerned with staff satisfaction than with serving the needy or when faculty become more concerned with gaining recognition for their scholarship from colleagues than with the education of students (which happens when promotions are geared to scholarship), then original goals are displaced. In bureaucracies, rules that were established to ensure quality control often become ends in themselves, with client outcomes sacrified on the alter of procedural regularity. Perhaps even more common is the shift from concern with program goals to organizational survival and maintenance goals. This may be appropriate if the original goals have been somehow met (as in the March of Dimes example), but it is hardly so when displacement leads to organizational sterility. Edward Banfield (1962) once pointed out that organizations are not like salmon, perishing in order to give birth to a new generation. They "much prefer sterility to death!"

Goal succession, expansion, and multiplication, on the other hand, may indicate signs of health, particularly when such changes are in response to new needs and opportunities. For example, when confronted with severe budget cuts in recent years, many community mental health centers shifted from heavy reliance on highly paid professional staff to community based on volunteer managed services. This often resulted in new forms of care and greater client involvement as both producers and consumers. Self-help, which had once been a goal of service, now became a means. Settlement houses and community centers, which had once perceived themselves as being in the business of Americanizing new immigrants (although they may have phrased it more delicately) are now directing many of their programs to building ethnic pride. The times have changed; and so have community perceptions of what is legitimate and what is not.

WHOSE GOALS?

Organizations, like all social systems, are shaped by forces in their external and internal environments. And these forces are often activated by parties with particular, even vested interests. Thus when federal or state policies and funding priorities shift, local agencies often modify their programs and services in the same directions to maintain legitimacy and to secure the resources they need to survive. If consumers can find alternative or better and cheaper services elsewhere, or if they are organized into advocacy groups, they too can exert pressures directly or indirectly through the market. If staff members can themselves legitimate the organization through the prestige associated with their professional status or technical skills, they too exert an influence on the organization's goals. There is much evidence of this in the medical field and in public education where prestigous practitioners set policy despite official authority being vested in boards and trustees representing community interests.

This suggests that organizations are likely to have multiple goals. Often these are associated with various organizational constitiences, each of which may be associated with particular functions; for example, those associated with boundary maintenance, production, management, and adaptation. Frequently, the goals arising from each function complement each other, although the danger always exists that the goal of one functional unit may come to inappropriately dominate those of other units. Thus, an inordinate focus on maintenance will divert resources and energy from production (service goals), *whereas* emphasis on current or original service goals may detract from an agency's ability to adapt to new conditions. It is important to remember what the agency originally set out to do, but we generally do so from the limited perspective of our own current interests in the organization. Oscar Wilde once pointed out that "conscience makes egotists of us all."

To understand an agency's real goals, in contrast with its stated goals, requires that we examine its operative goals. And that means looking near the bottom of the ends-means continum we described in our discussion of the branching tree approach. An agency's real goals are best uncovered by examining what it does, where resources are allocated, and who benefits from it all. I teach at the University of Michigan. A few miles down the road is Washtenaw Community College. Both have excellent reputations. Both define their general goals as contribution to knowledge, the education of students, and service to the society. But when we examine what they do, we discover that they are very different institutions indeed.

Scholarship at Michigan is paramount. Teaching is important, but easily takes a back seat to faculty research and publications. Service activities, if they generate research grants and student scholarships or larger state appropriations, may get some attention. Otherwise service receives only "lip service." At the community college, on the other hand, teaching and community service are paramount. Scholarship, if it is found, comes out of the individual instructor's hide.

GOALS AS THE DETERMINANT
OF AGENCY STRUCTURE

Goal analysis can also be useful in uncovering real versus presumed agency structure. If you cluster operative goals and means at the bottom end of the branching tree, you will find that they tend to parallel what we described in Chapter 4 as the agency's formal structure. But the fit won't be perfect. Look more closely, and you will find that each cluster also includes functional subsystems with the input and output relationships discussed in Chapter 5. Try charting these relationships. You may find yourself drawing ellipses around and across multiple clusters. If focusing on structure seems a bit static after our discussion of goals, keep in mind that structure is no more than agency processes viewed in a stable state. Process and activities are the organization structure viewed in a fluid state.

Before we conclude the discussion of organizational goals, A.A. Milne and I want to leave you with one thought. "Bump,

bump, bump, came Edward Bear, on the back of his head behind Christopher Robin. As far as he knew, this was the only way of coming downstairs. But sometimes he felt there really was another way, if only he could stop bumping for a while, to think of it.'

WHERE DOES THIS PERSPECTIVE LEAD YOU?

Among other things, if you view the agency as a goal seeking enterprise, you might:

— examine its operative goals so as to discover what relationships exists, if any, between the agency's stated and real goals;

— seek those places where important goals have been distorted or displaced;

— cluster goals and compare these clusters with the agency's formal structure, so as to make adjustments where needed to improve effectiveness and efficiency;

— identify those goals that continue to be functional as legitimators and guides to action and those that have become redundant and obsolete;

— find out whose goals really run the organization, and determine ways in which key interests (and interest groups) might better balance each other for the good of those who would suffer the most if the agency were to cease operating. Might these be its clients?

STRENGTHS AND LIMITS
OF USING THIS PERSPECTIVE

Strengths	Limits
Looking at the means-end continuum makes it possible to discover the real purposes of the agency.	Focusing on what the agency does may obscure what it does not do.
Clarity about goals increases the likelihood that agency resources will be appropriately directed. Clustering goals makes it possible to map both formal and functional relationships within the agency.	Those goals that are the most clear are likely to supersede other because rewards and penalties can be attached to achievement.
Examination of environmental (internal and external) pressures on agency purposes increases likelihood of shifting goals in response to changes in resources, expectations, and demands.	Overconcern with the environment may detract from ongoing commitment to the goals for which an agency or program was established.

Chapter 10

YOUR AGENCY AS A LOCUS OF POWER AND EXCHANGE RELATIONSHIPS

Throughout the book we have examined a variety of activities that individuals and organizations engage in order to achieve personal and organizational goals. These all involved some form of exchange, in which costs were borne and benefits sought. For social agencies to operate effectively, they must engage in multiple exchanges with their staff, with their clients and other consumers, and with those who provide legitimacy and other resources. To maintain an exchange relationship or to build on it requires a perception on the part of all concerned that the benefits outweigh the costs.

THE EXCHANGE RELATIONSHIP

Exchange is generally thought of as a rational process in which one party gives up something to another in order to gain a desired benefit to reward. This is true of economic exchanges in which both the costs and benefits can be measured. For example, in a simple economic exchange you might purchase a toaster, a course, or a program of counseling. You know what you are paying in time and money and you are presuming that the value of what you will receive will be worth the investment. The "seller" also has an investment in time, materials, and perhaps in opportunities lost (to sell to other customers or provide services to other clients). But the benefit in terms of income or satisfaction from fulfilling one's business or professional obligations is also perceived to outweight the costs. Thus, both parties to the exchange perceive some benefit, even though the benefits to each are not the same or even perhaps of equal weight. Moreover, the benefit gained need not be in the present. The course you have decided to enroll in may only pay off in new skills or new income earning ability some time in the future.

Exchanges occur between organizations as well as between people. In the chapter on environmental interactions we looked at interagency exchanges of an economic nature: the payments of fees for services by one organization to another, grants and contracts, joint efforts at assessment and program evaluation procedural integration, and the like. As in economic exchanges between individuals and between individuals and institutions (social agencies, retail stores), the costs are relatively easy to measure yet the benefits may not be. Social agencies, after all, are not in business to make profits. While cost reimbursement and containment are goals, other benefits are not likely to be so easily evaluated. If this is true of economic exchanges, it is all the more so of social exchanges.

The rewards and costs involved in social exchanges are rarely unambiguous. Social benefits do not have an exact price, since the utility of a given benefit cannot be clearly distinguished from that of other rewards derived from a particular relationship. For example, one can gain prestige and status from associating with prestigious people, but there may also be other rewards that have even greater meaning: the warmth of the friendship involved or the sense of well-being at being able to contribute to that relationship.

In the dating process, both parties involved may be seeking a rewarding relationship as well as some extrinsic benefits. In fact those extrinsics may be the basis upon which initial attraction was based: the prestige associated with being seen with an attractive person of the opposite sex; an opportunity to ride in a fancy car; the gratification expected from a good dinner; the cultural experience gained from attending a concert or play one would be embarrassed to attend on one's own. But as the parties to the exchange get to know each other, they may come to find the emerging relationship intrinsically rewarding.

At least part of the reward may come from relationships with third parties. A coed may initially be motivated to date a college football hero by the desire to "show the other girls what I can do" or to gain entry to a group of males with whom she would like to be associated. Thus there are some instrumental reasons for entering into the relationship, or, as we have termed it earlier, the expectation of some economic (clearly measurable) gains. This suggests a rather complicated set of relationships between economic and social exchanges that are both direct and indirect.

If you have engaged in fund raising or have contributed to the United Way or some other charitable organization, you will recognize what I am referring to. For example, if you have given a sizeable contribution to the UW, you may get some thanks from your solicitor, but you do not expect gratitude from the agencies who are to be the recipients of your gift (the real beneficiaries) or the clients of those agencies (the ultimate beneficiaries of this exchange process). Nevertheless, you are entitled to expect and to receive some return.

That return may be in the form of a tax exemption (instrumental or economic), an invitation to join the board (if you gift is especially big and consistently large from year to year), and the gratitude we spoke of earlier from the solicitor. That solicitor may be pleased, not only because of his or her concern for the agencies that will be more fully funded, but be also because "catching a big fish" accrues some prestige and recognition among fellow solicitors and campaign leaders (an expressive or social reward). You may benefit in the same way, increasing your prestige among colleagues and others who may be aware that you are one of the pacesetters in the community.

I'll cite another example that may be even closer to home. We all know big tippers whose motives are rarely what they claim (getting better or quicker service or "helping the waiter get a living wage"). The big tip may be more a function of impressing others at his or her table than of getting a return from the waiter.

These process are typical of all interactions between people and between people and other social units. Virtually all the interpersonal relationships we engage in within the agency and on its behalf are built around similar exchange processes. And all of them are based, at least initially, on some form of attraction. Think back on your first day at the agency. To whom were you attracted and what attracted you?

ATTRACTION AND ATTRACTIVENESS
AS SOURCES OF POWER

The concept of *attraction* bears some examination. It is generally used to explain the first stages of an exchange relationship. Attractive associates are persons who have impressed others as being rewarding to associate with. Such rewards may be perceived as extrinsic or intrinsic. Initially, the attraction of individuals to each other tends to rest more on extrinsic than on intrinsic factors. An interest in dating someone may be stimulated by how that person looks and with whom that person is associated, as well as by assumptions about impressing one's friends with having been seen with someone attractive. To get the first date the interested party may have to make him or herself attractive too. To make themselves attractive, people try to display those distinctive traits that are likely to impress others with the qualities that command admiration and respect. In any given situation these qualities might include such diverse elements as modesty, smart dress, intellectuality, suaveness, professional competence, curiosity, dominance, fragility, athletic prowess, and so on. It may even be expressed in terms of a need for help.

Coming back to your first day at the agency: Which of these qualities did you display? To whom? Did you sense a secretary had a need to do some mothering, so before her or him you appeared a bit flustered, in need of help? Did you sense that your supervisor expected a certain degree of self-confidence and professional know-how, so you made yourself appear on top of things? That would have been a natural and, in many circumstances, an appropriate response.

Consider also an experience you may have had in working on a staff committee or intergency task force. When the group was forming, did not at least some of the members attempt to impress others with their superior know-how, connections, previous accomplishments, or commitments to the group's mission, or perhaps with their willingness to do a great deal of work, even the group's dirty work? Nearly everyone needs to be appreciated. These people were trying to make themselves attractive to others, reasoning that by making themselves more attractive, they were likely to attract others, and with that attraction, meaningful exchanges might be possible.

You will have noticed that some members of the group may have been reluctant to appear overly attractive. Those impressive qualities that make one person particularly attractive may constitute a drain on their own personal resources and a status threat to others in the group. It is not unusual for those others to develop defensive postures, not allowing themselves to become too easily impressed. If one person (or one organization) possesses those qualities or resources that others need or desire, it gives them considerable power. Power is the potential to influence, and it is derived from exchange relationships. If one needs something, such as social recognition or help with performing unfamiliar tasks on a new job, one may have to be willing to subordinate oneself to another in order to receive the required service. Having accepted help, one becomes obligated to the helper.

By obligating another through an act of helping, one increases one's dominance over the other. That is why some individuals may resist certain exchange relationships, particularly those in which they seem to gain disproportionately. Nevertheless, the willingness of some participants in an association to subordinate themselves to an elected, appointed, or otherwise designated leader suggests their readiness to give up some of their own individual power for something else, perhaps the collective power that is the result of concentration.

This, as Weber (1933) pointed out in his classic work on bureaucracy, is one of the prime motivators in establishing complex organizations. Although power can be shared and concentrated, it tends always to be unevenly distributed because of the very nature of the exchange process. The concentration of power depends to a certain extent on the origins or derivation of that power (what it is based on) and in part on the extend to which others feel it is legitimately associated with certain individuals or organizations. Such legitimacy is dependent on the agreement of subordinates that more powerful individuals and organizations *should* hold power and that they are using it in a fair and equitable manner. Both the delegation of power and the acceptance of a subordinate position must be perceived as more beneficial (rewarding) than some other arrangement. Otherwise that legitimacy may be brought into question and the power relationships modified.

UNDERSTANDING POWER

Power is a value-laden term. For that reason, some persons shy away from its analysis. To have power or to be perceived

Chart 4

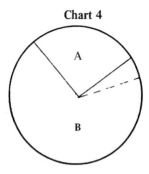

as powerful is to have the potential to influence others. Power refers to all the means by which individuals, groups, or institutions can exert controlling influence over others. And that reason it is sometimes suspect. For good reason; it can be corrupting if unbalanced or based on inappropriate sources. But power can be and generally is, used more positively. Like any other outcomes of an exchange relationship, power need not be defined in zero-sum terms; that is, a situation in which one party gains to the extent the other loses. When social workers, physicians, attorneys, and others band to establish a new service agency or a public interest campaign, they are concerting their potential to influence in ways that exceed their capacities as individuals working alone. When power is concerted and orchestrated, all sides can come up winners.

The following two charts will help you to understand a power differential in a relationship. When we say one person has power over another we do *not* mean that one person has power and the other person has none. We simply mean that one person has MORE power over the other person than the second has over the first.

In a win-lose situation, power is viewed as a fixed pie. The first chart indicates this and represents the amount of total power available. Person B has power since he or she has more power than A. The dotted line represents an increase in A's power that B will resist since any increase for A is a decrease in B's power.

Chart 5

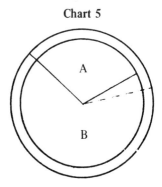

But power is described more accurately in the next chart in which it is viewed as a series of concentric circles. Viewed in this way, as new situations develop and A increases his or her power, B also increases his or her power. Thus, even giving up some power usually increases the amount B (in this case) has as well. B, after all, now has influence over A in the new situation as well as the remaining influence from what B previously maintained.

This perspective can be considered as complementary to the perspectives discussed earlier. For instance, developing relationships among elements in an environment involves consideration of the *types of influence* desired and the strategies used to attain them. Power or the potential to influence others is also used within an agency. It does not necessarily stem from one's status, nor is it restricted to one's role.

People lower in the hierarchy often have power over those higher up. Secretaries are excellent examples since they often have tremendous power over their bosses. People who have access to important information have the potential to influence others, even those above them in the hierarchy. Moreover, people who have access to important people can influence others. For example, the appointment secretary to the boss can often determine whether or not an individual is seen or heard. In interacting with that secretary, do so very carefully! Finally, people who have access to specific equipment tend to have power. Special physical therapy equipment may be needed to fulfill a client's needs. Whoever has access to it determines if *your* client's needs will be satisfied. These types of power tend to relate to position or location in an organization. Power can emanate from personal characteristics as well. For example, a staff member who is a therapist but who is also a strong emotional leader in an agency may have a very different (and perhaps more respected) kind of power than a program director who is efficient, but somewhat distant. The physical therapist has power to influence those seeking therapeutic assistance, and the client is willing to accept such influence because he or she perceives the therapist as having some knowledge or expertise from which a gain is possible. But the client is not without power. He or she can accept or reject help or reward or penalize the therapist through behavioral responses and affective relationships. Each person in your agency, and each of the actors in its environment (other agencies, funders, consumers as individuals or organized collectivities), can use power in some form to influence the behavior of others. To understand this more fully, it may help to describe different sources of power as they are used within social agencies and between them and others in the environment.

Keep in mind that these types of power are defined by the perceptions of the person being influenced, not the person with the alleged power. It really doesn't matter what type *you* think you have. The type of influence attributed to you depends on others' perceptions of you, of what *they* think you have (no matter how accurate).

The sources on which power is based include the ability to reward or to coerce, position in a hierarchy of authority, expertise, and mutual obligations. Let's take one at a time.

(1) *Reward* power is the potential to provide a desired benefit: a salary increase or promotion; a letter of recognition; referrals of clients; a grant or contract; the right to be associated with the person or organization giving the reward.

(2) *Coercive* power derives from the ability to withhold rewards or to apply negative sanctions. Social agencies can withhold benefits if clients do not comply with agency rules; some may even be able to apply legal sanctions (e.g., those associated with the courts or other elements in the justice system).

(3) Positional *authority* may derive from one's place on a hierarchy (e.g., department heads have authority over unit supervisors, federal courts have authority over district courts). Such positions are often derived from law or from organizational rules and regulations. They are generally formalized and clearly spelled out in agency manuals and the like.

(4) *Expert* power derives from technical competence or skill, which is presumed superior to those who are involved with the expert as subordinates in an exchange relationship. Clients presume expertise on the part of the caseworker: parents expect it of the school teacher; administrators of the management consultant, and so on.

(5) Power based on *mutual obligations* (sometimes called "referent power") is derived from personal relationships that over time generate a feeling of trust. One permits oneself to be influenced or is induced to act in certain ways if one knows that one can depend on the other to keep his or her side of a bargain or to provide a benefit when one is in need sometime in the future. It implies a sense of security that one can always call in one's cards at a future date. Trust grows with each successive and successful exchange.

Different circumstances may require different kinds of power. It would not be appropriate to use coercive tactics when approached for one's presumed expertise. The use of referent power in situations where positional authority is more appropriate might generate accusations of favoritism and nepotism. Whenever the wrong kind of power is used, its legitimacy comes into question. In part this is because inappropriate use of power suggests that one may not really have the power that was assumed. This is an important point to keep in mind. The type of influence attributed to you and your ability to use it is dependent on other's perceptions. Each of the types of power described above is determined by the perceptions of the persons subject to influence, not the persons with the alleged power.

The foregoing discussion is not meant to imply that only one kind of power should be applied in a given situation. To the contrary. It may be appropriate to use a combination of approaches: rewards, coercion, expertise, positional authority. Moreover, if one type does not seem to work (for example, mutual obligations in relating to a funding source), it may suggest that expert power would have been more appropriate all along. Take a few moments now to assess your own understanding of power relationships.

EXERCISE

Analyzing Power Relationships

Recall several situations at work in which you may have had influence over others because of your position, your ability to coerce or reward them, your expertise, or the mutual obligations you have built up over time. Describe one of these in detail.

Could you have reached your objective better if you had used a different tactic (power source) or by using a mix of tactics?

Now do a similar assessment of a situation in which someone used an inappropriate power source in an effort to influence your behavior. How did you react? How might you have reacted to influence their behavior in return? Would this have necessitated a direct transaction (exchange) with the offering party? Or would an indirect approach, working through others, have made more sense?

WHERE DOES THIS PERSPECTIVE LEAD YOU?

When you utilize this perspective, you might
— recognize what makes you attractive to others and what makes them attractive to you; engage in exchange relationships that are both direct and indirect, intrinsically and extrinsically rewarding;

— pay closer attention to lines of communication. All organizations find that they have people who control the flow of information. Pay particular attention to the use of referent power when coming into contact with them. Haul out your organizational chart. Mark points where you think communication occured and where it is blocked. Remember the person who controls the flow of information may not be the one who sits at the "top of the heap."

— pay close attention to people who control or have access to various key people or to key equipment;

— use what you have to get what you want. Everyone has some power. Be sure you understand what influence others have over you. KNOW the exchange and maximize it.

— transform a lack of power, especially as a representative of an organization, into a strength. This can be done by being unable to accept an influence attempt since your "constituents" in the agency won't accept that position.

STRENGTHS AND LIMITS
OF USING THIS PERSPECTIVE

Strengths	Limits
It allows for an honest assessment of influence types and sources and for rational problem solving in situations of competition that often lead to impulsive, irrational actions.	Relationships may be seen as competitive or even hostile when in fact they may only be uncoordinated or interacting in unproductive way.
Power analysis can help identify sites of influence within which leverage can be applied; understanding types of power can help determine what problem-solving attempts will be most effective.	When used without other perspectives as contexts, it may lead people to see their world being one in which power struggles are constantly occurring.
Especially in times of scarce resources, it can help maximize the resources available to an agency.	It can emphasize the competition for scant resources rather than cooperative and developmental strategies.
Being able to identify key power people, both within your agency and in other organizations in the task environment, is important if you want to avoid red tape and get work done.	

N O T E

1. I am indebted to Matt Lampe whose original draft of this chapter appeared in the first edition of *Understanding Your Social Agency*. The types of power discussed in this chapter are drawn from the work of John French and Bertram Raven (1968).

Chapter 11

A CONTINGENCY APPROACH TO PROBLEM-SOLVING IN THE AGENCY

We have concluded each of the preceding chapters with the question, "Where Does This Perspective Lead You?" and with a partial listing of the strengths and limits of each of the approaches described. In this chapter we'll explore how you might use each of these perspectives, alone or in tandem, to analyze an organizational problem and to design a solution to that problem.

We've looked at your agency as

(1) a *career arena* in which different worker-agency fits lead to alternative career styles;
(2) a system of *roles;*
(3) a system of norma and *small groups;*
(4) a system of *formal structures* that can be depicted on organizational charts;
(5) an *input-output processing* system that is functionally interdependent;
(6) interacting with key elements in its *environment;*
(7) a *people processing* and *people changing* system;
(8) the context within which *technologies* are applied;
(9) a *goal seeking* organization; and
(10) the locus of *exchange* and *power* relationships.

Our discussion of the strengths and limits of each perspective suggests that no one perspective will be useful in every situation. By using more than one perspective you can view an organizational problem from a number of vantage points. Alternative perspectives lead to alternative approaches to problem solving. This in itself may constitute an additional problem. You will now have to choose among perspectives and among alternative solutions to the problems you see.

If we could list every possible problem you are likely to encounter, it might be possible to indicate the most appropriate perspective to use. Of course this is not possible. No two human service agencies are exactly alike. A problem in one agency is not identical, although it may be similar to a problem in a second agency. For these reasons, I suggest using a "contingency approach." The contingency approach permits you to use more than one perspective for any given situation. As the situation changes, the perspectives used should also change.

To help you think through which perspectives might be appropriate to a given situation and in which order you might apply them, I've selected several fairly typical organizational problems to examine. Although each comes from a real life situation, I've chosen to describe each in fairly general terms so as to increase their universality. I think you will recognize these problems. All agencies face them. Discuss them with colleagues at your agency. They may agree or disagree with you on the perspectives you have chosen to apply. They may help you identify similar problems in your own agency. Collectively you may be able to arrive at some consensus regarding which perspectives to use and which of our alternative approaches to problem resolution make most sense.

Illustration 1: Not Reaching the Agency's Goals. Many agencies are faced with problems related to goal achievement. If your's is one, start by examining its *goal* structure. Are the operative goals related to the more general stated goals, those that legitemate the agency's efforts? Has there been goal displacement, distortion? Whose goals are dominant? How are *environmental* factors responded to? Do staff *career* interests or patterns impact on goals? Are the *technologies* used a major shaping factor? Have agency concerns with *input and output processing* (adaptation, boundary maintenance, management) distorted program goals?

This perspective may lead you to determine whether there are adequate resources and/or clients available to the agency or a department within it to accomplish desired goals. Focus on the effectiveness of the boundary system. What about the adaptive subsystem's ability to monitor changes in the environment. Have external elements in the task environment (e.g., new legislation, competitive services available from other agencies, changing client needs or demands) conspired to require an alteration of either goals or technology?

Assuming that you find the goals to be appropriate, you'll want to find out what it is that blocks goal attainment. Look inside the organization. Consider whether one of the following three perspectives is applicable. Viewing the organization as a career arena can provide you with information regarding leadership style, work climate, motivation, and the behavior of staff members in general. Do people know what is expected of them? Is there adequate feedback for staff on how they are progressing in relation to the organization's or work unit's goal? Is the leadership style employed consistent with the expectations of people working toward this goal?

Look also at the formal structure of your organization. Does the work or information flow in a manner that is consistent with requirements for goal attainment? By examining overlapping work groups the presence or absence of an integrated approach can be determined. Has the goal been properly transmitted downward? Has there been a mix-up in the reporting procedure? Are job descriptions sufficient to provide for task completion?

Finally try the input-output analysis. Look at the management, production, and boundary subsystems. Is the management subsystem providing the integrative and supportive assistance required? Is the survival of the agency still assured? Has the boundary subsystem provided all necessary resources? Is the production subsystem sufficiently efficient in the way it provides the services necessary to reach the goal? Assuming you've made the correct internal adjustments, but the agency's goals are still not being reached, another look outside the agency may be required. Examine the boundary and adaptive subsystems and the changes occurring in the environment of the agency. Understanding how the boundary subsystem works is as crucial as understanding how feedback works for the individual. Just as some staff members may not know what is expected of them, some organizations do not know exactly what is required of them. Is the organization fully aware of client needs or interests? Of funding requirements?

Illustration 2: Failure to Attract Clients. Consider the case of an agency that is unable to attract new clients at the same time it is facing a decline in demand by its existing client population. Survival may become a critical issue. Everybody agrees that the key person involved is the outreach worker (a boundary subsystem staff member) whose job it is to generate new clientele. He or she feels that the agency's rules and regulations are too restrictive and prevent fulfillment of assigned tasks. Besides, he or she is only one person and not a very powerful one at that. Having some expert power but *no* reward power with outside agencies from whom referrals might come is not very comforting. Nor is it easy to be without power over staff within the agency who might have to change the way in which they provide services if new clients are to be attracted.

At first, other staff members were inclined to agree that more outreach and intake staff were needed. Then they recognized that the source of the problem could be found mainly in the formal structure. After all, wasn't it the formal rules and procedures which put obstacles in the way of admitting clients to the agency? If this were true, the logical move is to alter agency rules, that is, to change the formal structure. But other possibilities exist.

Assume for the moment that rules are hard to change, that the formal structure is difficult to tamper with. Focus instead on the task environment. Perhaps a change can be made in that environment so as to alter the expectations of potential clients or increase their interest in the agency's services. Do clients select agencies on the basis of the perceived expert power of staff members? If so, promote that expertise. Help clients understand what agency staff workers can do for them.

The solutions suggested by this analysis is very different from the one originally proposed. Yet, both solutions follow logically from the perspective used. The perspective you choose has a tremendous impact on the way you define a problem and the alternative solutions you may find. This will be evident in the next illustration.

Illustration 3: Conflict. No organization can avoid conflict. It occurs both internally between members, groups or departments, and externally between an organization and others in its environment. When conflict is detrimental to the organization's ability to reach its goals, or to maintain itself, it requires some intervention.

An internal conflict occurred in a department of one agency which initially involved a superior and his subordinates, and ultimately the superior's boss. Using the "career arena perspective" and the "exchange and power perspective" adds more clarity than using the first perspective that may occur to you—the formal structure.

As subordinates, staff members could do very little through the formal hierarchy. Communication channels and reporting procedures indicated that all of the upward flow of information from the staff members was to go through the supervisor. The problem was that as a subordinate to the manager at the next level, he never transmitted the feelings and concerns of the staff members upward. Likewise, he communicated only a very distorted picture of top level directives to his subordinates. As the concerns of staff members increased, conflict increased until it was no longer tolerable either to the staff or the organization.

All staff members questioned his expertise ("expect power") His position was so threatened that few perceived him as having any reward power. Nevertheless, he *was* perceived as having both legitimate and coercive power. Using the personal perspective indicated that a tense climate existed and that an inappropriate leadership style was being applied by the manager. In addition, as the analysis progressed, it became obvious that the supervisor, a zealot who demanded personal loyalty to his sacred policies, had caused a division in his staff. One group became the "ins" and one the "outs." He would be confidential with the "ins" who supported his policies and almost totally exclude the other group from even limited communication.

What perspectives would you apply to this situation?

Some conflicts are induced externally. To better understand their origins, three perspectives seem to be especially helpful. The first examines the system's interaction with its environment. The set of organizations with which it interacts can determine, if not a solution, at least the likely sources of the conflict. Assuming this conflict is disadvantageous to the agency, having the adaptive subsystem monitor these organizations very closely can provide valuable information regarding an appropriate strategy to resolve the conflict.

Power relationships constitute a second way of looking at the problem. What sources of power is the agency perceived to have, and how can these be utilized to impact on the conflict situation? Who do you know in these other organizations who have access to people, equipment, or information? How can you influence these people?

The role perspective is also applicable, especially after isolating and identifying key people through the power perspective.

Use role set analysis to find an intervention approach. If you cannot influence these key people directly, how can you influence them indirectly? In other words, how can you influence the members in the role sets of those people whose behavior you want to modify?

Illustration 4: Implementing Change. Problem situations often emerge out of attempts to implement changes in an agency. As indicated in Chapter 6, the pressures for change are often generated by elements in the environment. Hence, using the environmental perspective and looking at the adaptive subsystem can be helpful in detecting where those pressures may come from. All of the remaining perspectives can also be brought into play. This is a situation where you have to look to all of them to determine which is the most productive in leading to a resolution of the problem. Take the larger problem and break it down into its subparts.

The major problem, for example, may be to overcome resistance to change. Looking into the people dimension allows you to categorize the persons most resistant. Are they conservers or zealots? Most people think that a conserver will be impossible to change because of his or her commitment to the status quo. But the conservers tend to do only what they are told. This means that they are unlikely to deviate from directions from above or from agency rules and procedures. By changing the rules and by getting the conserver's supervisor to instruct the conserver to abide by the new rules, resistance can be overcome.

Resistance to change may also stem from the fact that a change may break up a social group or put new and inappropriate demands on its members. Group members may fear that the proposed change will require that new services will have to be provided by the members. By coopting the group leader to support the proposed changes, resistance can be reduced. Getting group members to participate in the design of a conversion process (from current practices to those to be instituted) may lead to higher commitment to the new situation, thereby further reducing resistance. To get change accepted and implemented, you may have to go around an individual who is blocking the path for change. Examination of role sets and power relationships may be helpful.

One would not want to overlook the impact of new or changing technologies on the implementing of change. Which ones are available? Around which have vested interests consolidated? How are these technologies related to operative goals, the ones lower down on your branching tree?

USING THE CONTINGENCY APPROACH

Clearly, no single approach is adequate in fully understanding a problem or designing a solution for it. What I am suggesting is the progressive application of different points of view to a particular organizational problem. Each leads you to see a part of the problem that is otherwise hidden from view. Each may suggest a problem solution or a way of reducing the possible impact of that problem on the agency's survival and on the accomplishment of its service missions. Some problem solutions, however, may be blocked. Others may not be fully effective. Still others, when applied, may open up new problems.

In conclusion, I'd like to offer you the following tips:

(1) Use whatever perspective seems to shed some light and suggest one or more alternatives to overcoming or reducing the impact of a problem. If a perspective is not helpful after a point, drop it. Try another.

(2) Two or more perspectives are often applicable in any particular situation; so don't limit yourself to one at a time.

(3) For a particular situation, the use of different perspectives may lead to others. Don't press for a solution that has no chance of being implemented.

Now let's try to put it all together in a single exercise. It will help you be more systematic in your approach to organizational problem solving. Follow the steps outlined below.

STEP 1. PROBLEM DESCRIPTION

Identify a problem at work that is troubling you or the agency. Specify *what* it is, *who* is affected by it, *where* it is located, *when* it takes place (now, sometimes, all the time, in the near future, etc.), and *who else* is concerned or should be.

Leave some space to flesh out your description as you begin the contingency approach to problem analysis.

STEP 2. TENTATIVE PERSPECTIVE SELECTION

Which of the following perspectives do you think might most appropriately lead you to a solution of the problem or amelioration of the situation. Check all those that apply, giving a double check (✓✓) to the ones you think may be the most useful.

_____ 1. career arena

_____ 2. roles

_____ 3. small groups

_____ 4. formal structures

_____ 5. input-output

_____ 6. environment

_____ 7. people processing and people changing

_____ 8. technologies

_____ 9. goals

_____10. exchange and power

STEP 3. *ANALYZE THE PROBLEM USING DOUBLE-CHECKED PERSPECTIVES*

Starting with the perspectives you double-checked, analyze the problem in such a way as to lead you to a better understanding of its causes and consequences. Jot your notes down in as precise a manner as you can, using the language (concepts) you have been introduced to in the previous chapters.

STEP 4. ANALYZE THE PROBLEM USING ALTERNATIVE PERSPECTIVES

Now do the same using the other perspectives you checked. If these are not sufficient, which of the others you did not check might apply? Use them now.

STEP 5. *SELECTING FROM ALTERNATIVE PERSPEC-TIVES AND REFINING ANALYSIS*

Which of these perspectives do you find most helpful? Using them, describe the problem (from Step 1) in operational terms (drawing on your notes from Steps 3 and 4). Again, be as concrete as possible. And be brief. This is the form you might use in describing the problem in a proposal for action.

STEP 6. SPECIFYING OPERATIONAL OBJECTIVES

Describe your change objectives in operational terms. Refer to the relevant discussion in Chapter 9.

STEP 7. SPECIFYING ACTION ALTERNATIVES

Now specify the action alternatives that might be taken
to reach each of the objectives listed.

STEP 8. SELECTING FROM AMONG ALTERNATIVE ACTIONS

Finally, design a realistic action program. Select from among the alternatives listed under each objective in Step 7.

Select those alternatives on the basis of the following criteria:

— acceptability (to those most directly affected);

— resource availability (to implement the action);

— effectiveness (most likely to lead to goal achievement);

— least likely to have negative impact on other aspects of the agency's operations (and thus generate resistance).

Nice work! You've taken your first stab at organizational analysis and problem solving using the contingency approach. WHERE HAS THIS APPROACH LED YOU? WHAT ARE ITS STRENGTHS AND LIMITS? Which of these perspectives will you explore further? Put together a beginning reading list (check the references at the end of the book). With understanding comes responsibility. We all share it together in our efforts to improve our social agencies and the programs and services they provide.

REFERENCES

ABELS, P. and M.J. MURPHY (1981) Administration in the Human Services. Englewood Cliffs, NJ: Prentice-Hall.

ARGYRIS, C. (1954) Organization of a Bank. New Haven, CT: Yale University Press.

AUSTIN, D. (1981) "The political economy of social benefit organizations: Redistributive services and merit goods." In H. D. Stein (ed.) Organization and the Human Services: Cross-Disciplinary Reflections. Philadelphia: Temple University Press.

BANFIELD, E. C. (1962) "Ends and means in planning." In S. Mailick and E. H. van Ness (eds.) Administrative Behavior. Englewood Cliffs, NJ: Prentice-Hall.

BERNARD, C. (1938) The Functions of the Executive. Cambridge, MA: Harvard University Press.

von BERTALLANFFY, L. (1968) "General systems theory: A critical review." In W. Buckley (ed.) Modern Systems Research for the Behavioral Scientist. Chicago: Aldine.

BILLINGSLEY, A. (1967) "Bureaucratic and professional orientation patterns in social casework." Social Service Review 38 (December).

BLAU, P. (1975) Approaches to the Study of Social Structure. New York: Free Press.
———(1964) Exchange and Power in Social Life. New York: John Wiley.

BLUMER, H. (1962) "Society as symbolic interaction." In A. Rose (ed.) Human Behavior and Social Process. Boston: Houghton-Mifflin.

CARTWRIGHT, D. and A. ZANDER [eds.] (1968) Group Dynamics: Research and Theory. New York: Harper & Row.

CHURCHMAN, C. W. (1969) The Systems Approach. New York: Dell.

DOWNS, A. (1967) Inside Bureaucracy. Boston: Little, Brown.

DRUCKER, P. (1960) Concepts of the Corporation. Boston: Beacon Press.

EPSTEIN, I. (1970) "Professional role orientation and conflict strategies." Social Work 15 (October).

ETZIONI, A. (1964) Modern Organizations. Englewood Cliffs, NJ: Prentice-Hall.

EVAN, W. (1966) "The organization-set: Toward a theory of interorganizational relationships." In J. D. Thompson (ed.) Approaches to Organizational Design. Pittsburgh, PA: University of Pittsburgh Press.

FORM, W. H. and D. C. MILLER (1949) "Occupational career pattern as a sociological instrument." American Journal of Sociology 54 (June).

163

FRENCH, J. and B. RAVEN (1968) "The bases of social power." In R. Cartwright and A. Zander (eds.) Group Dynamics. New York: Harper & Row.

FRIEDSON, E. E. (1973) Professions and Their Prospects. Beverly Hills, CA: Sage.

GAMSON, W. (1968) Power and Discontent. Homewood, IL: Dorsey.

GOFFMAN, E. (1973) The Presentation of Self in Everyday Life. Garden City, NY: Doubleday.

GOULDNER, A. (1959) "Organizational analysis." In R. K. Merton et al. (eds) Society Today. New York: Basic Books.

GULICK, L. and L. URWICK (1937) Papers in the Science of Administration. New York: Columbia University Press.

HASENFELD, Y. (1972) "People processing organizations: An exchange approach." American Sociological Review 37 (June).

———and R. A. ENGLISH (1974) Human Service Organizations. Ann Arbor: University of Michigan Press.

HAWLEY, A. (1981) Urban Society: An Ecological Approach. New York: John Wiley.

HOMANS, G.C. (1958) "Social behavior as an exchange." American Journal of Sociology 63 (May).

———(1950) The Human Group. New York: Harcourt, Brace.

———and D. M. SCHNIEDER (1974) Social Behavior. New York: Harcourt, Brace, Jovanovich.

HUGHES, E. (1951) "Informal factors in career advancement." American Journal of Sociology 56 (March).

KATZ, D. and R. KAHN (1966) The Social Psychology of Organizations. New York: John Wiley.

LAUFFER, A. (1983) Grantsmanship (2nd ed.). Beverly Hills, CA: Sage.

———(1982) Getting the Resources You Need. Beverly Hills, CA: Sage.

———(1979) Resources for Child Placement and Other Human Services. Beverly Hills, CA: Sage.

LEAVETT, H. J. (1970) Managerial Psychology. Chicago: University of Chicago Press.

LEFTON, M. and W. R. ROSENGREN (1966) "Organizations and clients: Lateral and longitudinal dimensions." American Sociological Review 31 (December).

LEVINE, S. and P. E. WHITE (1961) "Exchange as a conceptual framework for the study of interorganizational relationships." Administration Science Quarterly 18 (March).

LEWIN, K. (1952) "Group decision and social change." In E. Maccoby and T. Newcombe (eds.) Readings in Social Psychology. New York: Holt, Rinehart, & Winston.

LINDBLOM, C. E. (1959) "The science of muddling through." Public Administration Review 19 (Spring).

LITTERER, J. A. [ed.] (1968) Organizations: Systems Control and Adaptation (vol. 2). New York: John Wiley.

LITWAK, E. and J. ROTHMAN (1970) "Toward the theory and practice of coordination between formal organizations." In W. R. Rosengren and M. Lefton (eds.) Organizations and Clients: Essays on the Sociology of Service. Columbus, OH: Bobbs-Merrill.

MARCH, J. G. and H. SIMON (1959) Organizations. New York: John Wiley.

McEWAN, W. J. and J. D. THOMPSON (1958) "Organizational goals and environ-
ment: Goal-setting as an interaction process." American Sociological Review 23
(February).
MERTON, R. K. (1964) Social Theory and Social Structure. New York: Free Press.
MOONEY, J. (1947) Principles of Organizations. New York: Harper Bros.
PARSONS, T. (1949) The Structure of Social Action. New York: Macmillan.
————E. SHILS, K. D. NAEGELE, and J. R. PITTS [eds.] (1961) Theories of
Society. New York: Free Press.
PATTI, R. (1975) "The new scientific managment: Systems management for social
welfare." Public Welfare 33 (Spring).
PERROW, Charles G. (1965) "Hospitals: Technology, structure, and goals." In
J. G. March (ed.) Handbook of Organizations. Chicago: Rand McNally.
————(1961) "The analysis of goals in complex organizations." American Sociological
Review 26.
PROTTAS, J. M. (1980) People Processing. Lexington, MA: D. C. Heath.
SARRI, R. C. and Y. HASENFELD (1978) The Management of Human Services.
New York: Columbia University Press.
SAYLES, L. R. (1955) Research in Industrial Human Relations. New York: Harper Bros.
SELZNICK P. (1943) "An approach to a theory of bureaucracy." American Sociological
Review 8 (January).
SIMON, H., D. W. SMITHBURG, and V. A. THOMPSON (1950) Public Administra-
tion. New York: Macmillan.
STINCHCOMBE, A. (1968) Constructing Social Theories. New York: Harcourt,
Brace, Jovanovich.
STREET, D., R. D. VINTER, and C. PERROW (1966) Organization for Treatment.
New York: Free Press.
TAYLOR, F. (1911) Scientific Management. New York: Harper Bros.
THOMPSON, J. D. (1967) Organizations in Action. New York: McGraw-Hill.
————R. O. CARLSON, and R. W. AVERY (1968) "Occupations, personnel, and
careers." Educational Administration Quarterly (Winter).
THOMPSON, J. D. and W. J. McEWAN (1958) "Organizational goals and environ-
ment: Goal setting as an interaction process." American Sociological Review 23
(February).
VINTER, R. D. (1963) "Analysis of treatment organizations." Social Work 8 (July).
WEBER, M. (1970) "Bureaucracy." In O. Grusky and G. Miller (eds.) The Sociology
of Organizations. New York: Free Press
WHYTE, W. F. (1951) "Small groups in large organizations." In J. Rohrer and
M. Sherif (eds.) Social Psychology at the Crossroads. New York: Harper Bros.
ZANDER, A.F., A. R. COHEN, and E. STOTLAND (1957) Role Relations in
the Mental Health Professions. Ann Arbor: University of Michigan Press.

ABOUT THE AUTHOR

ARMAND LAUFFER is Professor of Social Work at the University of Michigan, where he teaches courses in administration, staff development, and community planning. He received his doctorate at Brandeis University and has spent several years on the faculties of the Hebrew University and Haifa University in Israel as a visiting professor.

Editor of the Sage Human Service Guides, Lauffer has written a number of other professional books.

For Sage:

Grantsmanship and Fundraising, 1984
Grantsmanship (2nd edition), 1983
Assessment Tools, 1982
Getting the Resources You Need, 1982
Health Needs of Children (with Roger Manela), 1979
Resources for Child Placement, 1979
Volunteers (with Sarah Gorodezky), 1977
Understanding Your Social Agency (1st edition, with Lynn Nybell, Carla Overberger, Beth Reed, and Lawrence Zeff), 1977
Grantsmanship (1st edition), 1977

Other books in print:

Strategic Marketing for Not-for-Profit Organizations, 1984
Community Organization for the 1980s (ed. with Edward Newman), 1982

Doing Continuing Education and Staff Development, 1978
Social Planning at the Community Level, 1978
The Practice of Continuing Education in the Human Services, 1977
The Aim of the Game, 1973
Community Organizers and Social Planners (with Joan L. Ecklein), 1972.